MOMENTS WITH MAMA KATIE

Katie Brown

Birdge Builder Books Bublishing LLC

Cover design by: Celeste Easter
Printed in the United States of America

*This book is dedicated to all who seek solace and strength
in their moments of solitude and to those who gather
in communion, thirsting for spiritual nourishment and
companionship along their journey. May these pages serve as a
bridge connecting hearts across the divides of experience and
circumstance.*

*To my children, grandchildren, and great-grandchildren,
who have taught me the depth of unconditional love and
the strength that lies in vulnerability, thank you for inspiring
every word with your light and your challenges. To my beloved
community, who has walked with me through seasons of both
bounty and barrenness, your support has been my anchor and
your needs my compass.*

*Above all, to our Heavenly Father, who entrusts us with His
wisdom and guides us with His gentle, steadfast hand. May
this humble offering reflect the beauty of His holiness and the
boundless reach of His love.*

*May you find, within these pages, wisdom that resonates and
truths that empower. Walk this path with me, and together, let
us grow in the grace and knowledge of our Lord.*

With all my love and prayers,

Mama Katie

CONTENTS

The Adventure Beneath Our Feet

DAY 1: DAILY DEVOTION
THE SPIRIT OF KNOWLEDGE AND
OF THE FEAR OF THE LORD

W hat a remarkable opportunity we've been granted to be the bedrock of faith, walking steadfastly in the journey of life. Isaiah 11:2 speaks of the divine attributes instilled within us by the Holy Spirit—wisdom, understanding, counsel, might, knowledge, and reverence for the Lord.

Reflecting on "the spirit of knowledge and of the fear of the Lord," Proverbs 2:10 resonates deeply: "An intelligent heart acquires knowledge, and the ear of the wise seeks knowledge." Through our interactions with others, filled with prayer, laughter, and shared moments, we earnestly seek the wisdom needed for our path ahead.

In 2 Timothy 1:7, we find solace, knowing that God has blessed us with power, love, and a sound mind, dispelling any fears that may arise. Our reverence for the Lord, as echoed in Psalm 111:10, serves as the cornerstone of true wisdom, guiding us in following His commands and gaining understanding.

To walk out our Christian faith authentically, we must nurture a close bond with the Holy Spirit, allowing His Word to transform us from the inside out. As we are shaped by His truth, we become vessels through which His love and wisdom flow, impacting the lives of those we encounter daily.

John 5:39 reminds us that the Scriptures bear witness to Jesus, the embodiment of God's love and redemption for humanity. Our reverence for God stems not from fear of judgment, but from awe of His greatness, His steadfast love, and His unchanging nature.

Ecclesiastes 12:13 encapsulates the essence of our devotion: to fear God and keep His commandments, for this is the duty of every person. Let us draw near to Him, immersing ourselves in His Word and embracing His promises, knowing that all His promises are Yes and Amen. May all glory be unto our faithful God, who leads us in paths of righteousness and abundance.

Day 1 - Journaling Activity:
Walking in Faith

Reflect on Scripture: Take a moment to read and meditate on Isaiah 11:2, Proverbs 2:10, 2 Timothy 1:7, Psalm 111:10, John 5:39, and Ecclesiastes 12:13. Consider how these verses speak to you personally and what insights they offer about walking in faith.

Personal Reflection: Write about a time when you felt the presence of the Holy Spirit guiding you or giving you wisdom in a challenging situation. How did you respond? What did you learn from the experience?

Seeking Knowledge: Reflect on the concept of seeking knowledge with an open heart and mind, as mentioned in Proverbs 2:10. Think about areas of your life where you desire more understanding or wisdom. Journal about specific steps you can take to seek knowledge in those areas.

Fear of the Lord: Explore your understanding of the fear of the Lord as described in Psalm 111:10 and Ecclesiastes 12:13. Consider what it means to reverence God and how this reverence influences your daily life and decisions.

Applying Wisdom: Think about practical ways you can apply the wisdom and insights gained from your study of Scripture to your everyday life. Write down action steps or commitments to integrate these principles into your thoughts, words, and actions.

Gratitude and Praise: Close your journaling session by expressing gratitude to God for His faithfulness, wisdom, and love. Write a prayer or a poem praising God for His unchanging nature and for the assurance that all

His promises are Yes and Amen.

DAY 2: WEEK 1 DEVOTION

EMBRACING GRATITUDE EVERY DAY

The suggestion to maintain a gratitude journal might initially seem like well-trodden advice, yet its power and significance cannot be overstated. My personal journey with journaling has profoundly demonstrated its value. On those challenging days—when our spirits waver and we find ourselves questioning, "Where are you, God?"—it's the practice of reflecting on our journals that brightly illuminates the myriad ways the Holy Spirit has subtly communicated with us, gently preparing and guiding us through life's hurdles.

As we cultivate a spirit of thanksgiving, let's broaden our perspective beyond the annual holiday to embrace gratitude every single day. This mindset shift ushers in a realization: we don't need to wait for a special occasion to count our blessings or to acknowledge the divine workings in our lives and those around us.

Today, let's stand united in this journey of daily thanksgiving, drawing inspiration from Ezekiel 36:25-26. With heartfelt conviction, let's affirm, "I will sprinkle clean water on you, and you will be clean; from all your impurities and from all your idols, I will cleanse you. I will give you a new heart and put a new spirit within you; I will take from you your heart of stone and give you a heart of flesh." This scripture encourages us to believe in the transformative power of God's love, not just for ourselves but also for our loved ones, anticipating a renewal of heart that every day can bring.

As we navigate our daily lives, let's do so with the awareness that God's work is ever-present. Let the fruits of the Spirit—love, joy, peace, patience, kindness, goodness, faithfulness, gentleness, and self-control—embrace us fully. In each moment, let's remember that our prayers are heard, our concerns are known, and no challenge is too daunting for His capable hands. May this spirit of daily thanksgiving fill your heart, shining a light on the everyday blessings that surround us, and reinforcing the belief that every day is an opportunity to live in the fullness of God's grace and love.

Day 2: Week 1 -Journaling Activity
Embracing Daily Gratitude

In harmony with the spirit of our devotion, this journaling activity is designed to deepen your daily practice of gratitude, ensuring it becomes a cherished part of your routine. By engaging with this activity, you'll create a tangible record of God's presence and blessings in your life, nurturing a heart that sees every day as a day of Thanksgiving.

Recognizing the Divine in the Daily

Day 1: Reflections of Gratitude

- Start your journal entry by listing three simple joys you experienced today. Reflect on how these moments felt and consider the ways they might reveal God's grace in your life.

Day 2: God's Whispers

- Write about a time today when you felt a sense of peace, comfort, or guidance that you attribute to the Holy Spirit. Describe the situation and how it influenced your day.

Day 3: Lessons Learned

- Journal about a challenge you faced today. Reflect on what you learned from it and how it might be preparing you for future blessings.

Day 4: Scripture and Serenity
● Choose a verse from the Bible that speaks to you today. Write it down and explore why it resonates with you at this moment.

Day 5: Acts of Kindness

- Reflect on an act of kindness you received or offered today. How did this exchange of goodwill remind you of God's love?

Day 6: Prayerful Petitions

- Write a prayer for a friend or family member, asking God to renew their heart and spirit. Reflect on the power of intercessory prayer in your life.

Day 7: Sabbath Reflections

- Spend today's journaling session reflecting on the past week. Note any patterns or recurring themes in your entries. How has focusing on daily gratitude affected your outlook?

Integrating Gratitude Into Daily Life

- Gratitude Reminders: Set daily reminders to pause and note something you're grateful for, even on busy days.
- Gratitude Sharing: Once a week, share a highlight from your journal with a friend or family member. This act of sharing can multiply gratitude and encourage others to reflect on their own blessings.

- Reflective Walks: Incorporate a weekly gratitude walk into your routine, using the time to reflect on the blessings in your life and the beauty of God's creation around you.

Through this journaling activity, you'll not only cultivate a deeper sense of gratitude but also forge a more intimate connection with God, recognizing His loving presence in every aspect of your daily life.

WEEK 2 - WEEKLY DEVOTION
FINDING SANCTUARY IN FAITH

This morning, as I turned the pages of my YouVersion Bible app to the verse of the day, Psalm 27 beckoned to me with a divine whisper. The Holy Spirit urged, "Pause and Park Here." Immersed in the depth of Psalm 27, it dawned upon me: the fullness of His promises is accessible to us in every word. Whatever challenges or fears we face—be it loneliness, worry, doubt—imagine inserting them directly into this Psalm. Their power diminishes in the light of His strength.

Recently, our Pastor shared wisdom on mastering our thoughts, highlighting that while we cannot prevent certain thoughts from entering our mind, we possess the power to decide which ones we entertain and nurture. He introduced us to the TSA method for thoughts:
T - Take authority over your thoughts by asserting your control.
S - Sit down with your thoughts, engaging them with questions like, "What's your name?", "Where did you come from?", and "Where are you going?"
A - Analyze your thoughts, embracing those that uplift and align with God's truth.

As you read Psalm 27, listen attentively for the Holy Spirit's voice, offering you solace and strength. Step into His sanctuary —a place of refuge, shelter, and unconditional love.

Psalm 27 of David – (NIV)

The Lord is my light and my salvation—whom shall I fear? The Lord is the stronghold of my life—of whom shall I be afraid?

When the wicked advance against me to devour me, it is my enemies and my foes who will stumble and fall.

Though an army besiege me, my heart will not fear; though war break out against me, even then I will be confident.

One thing I ask from the Lord, this only do I seek: that I may dwell in the house of the Lord all the days of my life, to gaze on the beauty of the Lord and to seek him in his temple.

For in the day of trouble he will keep me safe in his dwelling; he will hide me in the shelter of his sacred tent and set me high upon a rock.

Then my head will be exalted above the enemies who surround me; at his sacred tent I will sacrifice with shouts of joy; I will sing and make music to the Lord.

Hear my voice when I call, Lord; be merciful to me and answer me.

My heart says of you, "Seek his face!" Your face, Lord, I will seek.

Do not hide your face from me, do not turn your servant away in anger; you have been my helper. Do not reject me or forsake me, God my Savior.

Though my father and mother forsake me, the Lord will receive me.

Teach me your way, Lord; lead me in a straight path

because of my oppressors.

Do not turn me over to the desire of my foes, for false witnesses rise up against me, spouting malicious accusations.

I remain confident of this: I will see the goodness of the Lord in the land of the living.

Wait for the Lord; be strong and take heart and wait for the Lord.

In the embrace of these verses, find the courage to face each day with a heart fortified by faith, knowing you are sheltered within the vastness of His love and promises.

Week 2 - Journaling Activity:
Discovering Your Sanctuary in Faith

This journaling activity is crafted to accompany your reflection on Psalm 27, encouraging a deeper engagement with the themes of refuge, strength, and the presence of God in your life. As you embark on this journey, allow each prompt to guide you into a more intimate dialogue with your faith and the divine whispers that seek to comfort and guide you.

Day 1: Identifying Your Fears

- Reflect on the fears and challenges currently present in your life. Write them down as if you are naming your adversaries. How do these fears compare to the assurance found in Psalm 27:1-2?

Day 2: Authority Over Thoughts

- Practice the TSA method with your thoughts from yesterday. Take authority, Sit down with them, and Analyze. Journal about this experience and any revelations that emerged.

Day 3: Seeking His Presence

- Reflect on Psalm 27:4. What does it mean to you to dwell in the house of the Lord all your days? How can you seek His presence in your daily life?

Day 4: God's Protection

- Recall a time when you felt God's protection, akin to being sheltered in His sacred tent as described in Psalm 27:5. Write about this experience and how it affected your faith.

Day 5: Joy and Worship

- Psalm 27:6 speaks of offering sacrifices with shouts of joy and making music to the Lord. Create a list of things you are thankful for and ways you can express your joy and worship in everyday life.

Day 6: Seeking His Face

- Meditate on the words, "My heart says of you, 'Seek his face!' Your face, Lord, I will seek" (Psalm 27:8). Journal about what seeking God's face looks like in your life. How do you feel called to pursue a deeper relationship with Him?

Day 7: Confidence in His Promises

- Reflect on the confidence David proclaims in Psalm 27:13-14. Write a letter to yourself from the perspective of having seen the goodness of the Lord in the land of the living. What words of encouragement and hope would you offer?

Weekly Reflection

At the end of the week, review your journal entries and reflect on how engaging with Psalm 27 has impacted your view of God as your refuge and strength. What changes do you notice in your feelings of fear or doubt? How has your understanding of seeking God's face deepened?

Creating Your Sanctuary

As an extension of this activity, consider creating a physical or digital "sanctuary" where you can continue to explore your faith and feelings. This could be a dedicated journal, a folder on your computer, or a special space in your home where you can sit, reflect, and write. Fill this sanctuary with reminders of God's promises to you, including verses from Psalm 27, to continually renew your spirit and strengthen your faith.

Through these journaling prompts and the creation of your sanctuary, may you find a deeper sense of peace and assurance in God's eternal presence and protection.

WEEK 3 - WEEKLY DEVOTION
SEEKING GOD IN EVERY STEP

Reflecting on last week's devotion, we unearthed precious insights about the essence of living a life aligned with God's will—seeking, listening, and then acting. This week, let's delve deeper into the posture we assume in the face of adversity, inspired by the profound narratives found in 2 Chronicles 20:1-39 and the strategic inquiries of David in 1 Chronicles 14:13-17.

When confronted with unsettling news or disheartening words, what's your instinctive reaction? Do we buckle under the weight of fear, or do we mirror Jehoshaphat's unwavering faith, turning our first and most earnest appeals towards God? It's all too easy to be swept up in the whirlwind of distractions, losing sight of our divine anchor and the omnipotence of our Creator. These distractions can blur our vision, making us forget our identity and the powerful legacy we inherit as children of God.

In the scriptures, we're reminded of David's exemplary leadership and devout reliance on God's guidance. Faced with the threat of the Philistines, David didn't rush into battle with human strategy alone; he sought God's direction. And God's response was precise and strategic, leading to a resounding victory that echoed throughout the lands, elevating David's renown and instilling a divine fear among the nations.

These narratives underscore a timeless truth: the importance of seeking God first, irrespective of the situation's magnitude.

Every trial we encounter is an opportunity for triumph, a chance to witness God's victorious might firsthand. He has never faced defeat and promises the same victory to those who align with Him.

Let's make a conscious decision to seek His counsel before responding to any challenge. Before we assert our plans or declare our capabilities, let's pause and pray, inviting God to steer our intentions and actions. This commitment to divine alignment promises not only personal transformation but also a positive impact on our surroundings—our families, workplaces, and communities.

Philippians 1:6 reassures us, "Being confident of this very thing, that he who began a good work in you will carry it on to completion until the day of Christ Jesus." This promise is a beacon of hope, affirming that the work God has started in us will be faithfully executed to its glorious fruition.

Today, let's embrace a lifestyle of continuous seeking, listening, and responding to God's voice. As we align our steps with His guidance, we'll witness transformative changes within and around us, proving that when we put God first, the impossible becomes possible.

Week 3 - Journaling Activity:
Aligning with God in Every Step

This journaling activity is designed to complement your journey through the devotion "Seeking God in Every Step." It aims to deepen your reflection on seeking God's guidance in the face of adversity and in making decisions. By engaging with these prompts, you'll explore your reactions to challenges, recognize the importance of consulting God first, and understand how this practice can transform your life and those around you.

Day 1: Reflection on Reactions

- Reflect on a recent situation where you received unsettling news or faced a challenge. Write down your initial reaction and compare it with Jehoshaphat's response in 2 Chronicles 20:1-39. What could you learn from his example?

Day 2: Distractions and Identity

- Identify distractions that tend to lead you away from remembering who you are in God and to whom you belong. Journal about ways to overcome these distractions and refocus on God's power and might.

Day 3: Seeking God's Guidance

- Think about a decision you need to make or a challenge you're currently facing. Spend time in prayer, seeking God's guidance. Afterwards, journal about the experience and any insights or directions you felt God provided.

Day 4: The Power of Inquiry

- Reflect on David's strategy of inquiring of the Lord before action, as described in 1 Chronicles 14:13-17. Write about a situation where you could apply this approach. How might seeking God first change the outcome?

Day 5: Impact of Our Words

- Consider the power of your words and their impact on your environment. Before you speak today, take a moment to pray and inquire of the Lord. At the end of the day, journal about any changes you noticed in your interactions and their outcomes.

Day 6: Transformation Through Seeking God

- Reflect on the changes you want to see in your circle of influence, your family, co-workers, and fellow believers. How can seeking God first lead to transformation in these areas? Write down specific prayers for each area.

Day 7: Embracing the Promise

- Meditate on Philippians 1:6. Write a letter to yourself from the perspective of your future self, looking back on how seeking God first has completed the good work He began in you. What accomplishments and transformations do you see?

Weekly Reflection:

At the end of the week, review your journal entries and reflect on how this practice of seeking God first has begun to transform your perspective and approach to challenges. Consider setting aside time for a monthly or quarterly review of this journaling activity to track your growth and adjustments in your spiritual journey.

This journaling activity is intended to be a personal retreat, a time for you to engage deeply with your faith and the practical application of living a life aligned with God's will. May it serve as a catalyst for profound spiritual growth and transformation.

WEEK 4 - WEEKLY DEVOTION
EMBRACING THE SPIRIT OF
ADVENT BEYOND THE SEASON

In the quiet moments following the Thanksgiving celebrations, my thoughts wandered to the profound meaning of the upcoming Advent season—a period of spiritual reflection and preparation that transcends denominational boundaries. It's a time to meditate on the powerful truth declared in Luke 2:11, "For unto you is born this day in the city of David a Savior, who is Christ the Lord."

The essence of Advent lies not just in the anticipation of Christmas but in the year-round journey of embodying the light and love of Christ. It reminds us of the joy and gratitude that fills our hearts as we contemplate God's ultimate gift to humanity: His Son, sent to redeem us. John 1:14 beautifully encapsulates this gift, "The Word became flesh and made his dwelling among us. We have seen his glory, the glory of the one and only son," bridging the joyous celebration of Jesus's birth with the profound sacrifice of His crucifixion. It's a testament to God's immense love for us, offering daily opportunities to experience His grace and reflect His glory.

The saying "Jesus Is the Reason for the Season" should not be confined to the weeks leading up to Christmas. If Jesus is truly at the heart of our celebrations, then love, joy, and peace should permeate our lives throughout the year. These virtues, which Jesus exemplified, can transform every season into a reflection of the joy and redemption His birth brings.

Advent invites us to live in expectancy and excitement for what God has done and continues to do. It's a reminder that we are chosen to represent an incredible God every day. We are His ambassadors, tasked with sharing His glory and love with the world.

As we move beyond the Advent season, let's carry its spirit with us every day. Let this time of preparation and reflection inspire us to live in a way that honors Jesus, not just during Advent but throughout the entire year. By doing so, we make our lives a continuous celebration of the hope, joy, and redemption found in Christ. Remember, you are chosen to be a beacon of His light and love in this world—embrace this calling with joy and gratitude every day.

Week 4 - Journaling Activity: Living the Spirit of Advent Every Day

This journaling activity is designed to accompany the devotion on carrying the spirit of Advent beyond the season, helping you to deeply internalize and practice the essence of Advent—joy, anticipation, preparation, and reflection—throughout the entire year.

Day 1: Reflection on the Incarnation

- Meditate on Luke 2:11 and John 1:14. Reflect on the significance of the incarnation of Jesus, God becoming flesh. How does this truth impact your daily life and perspective?

Day 2: Gratitude for Divine Love

- Consider the profound love God demonstrated through Christ's birth and sacrifice. Write a letter of gratitude to God, acknowledging His love and what it means to you personally.

Day 3: Joy in Jesus

- "Jesus Is the Reason for the Season" is a popular saying that highlights the joy of Advent. How can you maintain this joy in your heart throughout the year? Identify specific ways to cultivate joy in your daily life.

Day 4: Everyday Peace

- Jesus is our Prince of Peace. Reflect on how you can embody and spread His peace in your everyday interactions. Are there areas in your life where you need to seek His peace more earnestly?

Day 5: Love in Action

21

- Love is the central theme of Jesus's teachings. Journal about practical ways you can show love to those around you every day. How can you make love a more intentional part of your daily routine?

Day 6: Anticipation and Hope

- Advent is a season of anticipation for the coming of Christ. How can you live in a state of hopeful anticipation for God's work in your life and the world around you? Reflect on the aspects of your life where you need to cultivate more hope.

Day 7: Reflection and Preparation

- Advent is also a time for reflection and preparation. What spiritual practices can you incorporate or strengthen in your life to stay spiritually prepared and reflective throughout the year?

Weekly Reflection:

At the end of the week, review your journal entries. Reflect on how integrating the spirit of Advent into your daily life changes your perspective, actions, and interactions. Consider setting goals based on your reflections to help you carry the essence of Advent with you every day.

Continuous Journey:

Commit to revisiting these journaling prompts quarterly or whenever you need a reminder of the spirit of Advent. This continuous engagement will help you maintain a heart of joy, anticipation, and reflection, allowing you to truly live out the message and meaning of Advent every day of the year.

DAILY DEVOTION
DAY CULTIVATING A VISION OF
FAITH: FIXED EYES VS. GAZING

In the heartwarming narrative of Acts 3:1-8, we witness a miraculous moment between Peter, John, and a man lame from birth. This story beautifully illustrates the power of fixed faith and the transformative miracles that can occur when our eyes are truly focused on God and His promises.

The encounter at the temple gate called Beautiful becomes a vivid tableau of expectation versus divine intervention. The lame man, positioned daily to beg, sees Peter and John and anticipates mere monetary aid. Yet, what unfolds is a testament to a greater provision—the healing power found in the name of Jesus Christ of Nazareth. This miracle, prompted by a faith that looks beyond the physical and material, invites us to examine the focus of our own faith. Are we merely glancing at God's promises, seeking temporary solace, or are we fixing our gaze, fully assured in the truth of His Word?

Fixed eyes do not waver in the face of uncertainty or adversity. They understand the immutable nature of God—"the same yesterday, today, and forever" (Hebrews 13:8). This steadfast gaze recognizes no boundaries to what can be achieved through divine will and power.

> •Fixed eyes know there are no limits to what the Father can do in and through you.
> • Fixed eyes know that no weapon formed against you shall prosper.
> •Fixed eyes know God says He created the weapons that are formed.
> •Fixed eyes know He is able to destroy and demolish every stronghold that comes against you.
> •Fixed eyes know He made you an overcomer.
> •Fixed eyes know that the greater one lives *on* the inside of you.
> •Fixed eyes know they can run and not get weary.
> •Fixed eyes know that they are fearfully and wonderfully made.
> •Fixed eyes know that they are God's masterpiece.

Conversely, gazing eyes flit from one solution to another, surprised by God's faithfulness and quick to doubt when miracles seem delayed. They miss the depth of conviction found in 2 Timothy 1:12: "I know whom I have believed, and am convinced that he is able to guard what I have entrusted to him until that day."

Today, let us choose to fix our eyes firmly on the Triune God, immersing ourselves in the promises woven throughout His Word. Embrace the vision of faith that knows God is "able to do immeasurably more than all we ask or imagine" (Ephesians 3:20). Let this conviction guide your path, transform your heart, and renew your mind, so that every step you take is anchored in the certainty of His eternal love and power. Amen.

Daily - Journaling Activity:
Walking in Faith

Reflect on Scripture: Take a moment to read and meditate on Isaiah 11:2, Proverbs 2:10, 2 Timothy 1:7, Psalm 111:10, John 5:39, and Ecclesiastes 12:13. Consider how these verses speak to you personally and what insights they offer about walking in faith.

Personal Reflection: Write about a time when you felt the presence of the Holy Spirit guiding you or giving you wisdom in a challenging situation. How did you respond? What did you learn from the experience?

Seeking Knowledge: Reflect on the concept of seeking knowledge with an open heart and mind, as mentioned in Proverbs 2:10. Think about areas of your life where you desire more understanding or wisdom. Journal about specific steps you can take to seek knowledge in those areas.

Fear of the Lord: Explore your understanding of the fear of the Lord as described in Psalm 111:10 and Ecclesiastes 12:13. Consider what it means to reverence God and how this reverence influences your daily life and decisions.

Applying Wisdom: Think about practical ways you

can apply the wisdom and insights gained from your study of Scripture to your everyday life. Write down action steps or commitments to integrate these principles into your thoughts, words, and actions.

Gratitude and Praise: Close your journaling session by expressing gratitude to God for His faithfulness, wisdom, and love. Write a prayer or a poem praising God for His unchanging nature and for the assurance that all His promises are Yes and Amen.

WEEK 5 - WEEKLY DEVOTION
EMBARKING ON THE JOURNEY
TO WHOLENESS

In the poignant narrative of John 5:6, we find Jesus extending an invitation that echoes through the ages to each of us today: "Will you be made whole?" This question, directed towards a man who had been waiting for healing for an extended period, resonates deeply with our own experiences of waiting and yearning for change.

Much like the man at the Bethesda pool, we too can find ourselves entangled in excuses for why we haven't yet embraced the wholeness Jesus offers. It's easy to claim that the hustle of daily life leaves little room for spiritual growth or to become so accustomed to our struggles that they become a part of our identity. Yet, Jesus, with compassion and authority, cuts through these excuses, urging us, "Get up! Pick up your mat and walk" (John 5:8).

Jesus's command is a powerful call to action for us today. He invites us to lift up the Word of God as our foundation for healing and transformation. By immersing ourselves in Scriptures that speak to our specific needs, we arm ourselves with divine truths capable of dismantling the lies of the enemy. The Word of God stands as our indefatigable weapon for ushering in change in our lives, promising wholeness in body, soul, and spirit.

Jesus's earthly journey was marked by experiences of pain,

temptation, and suffering, yet He triumphed over each, offering Himself as a beacon of hope for our own journey towards healing. He beckons us to step into the fullness of life He has secured for us, a life where His love and sacrifice render us complete.

As Apostle Paul instructed Timothy, delving into the Scriptures is not merely an academic exercise but a quest for divine approval and understanding (2 Timothy 2:15). The Scriptures are a testament to Jesus's completed work on the Cross, revealing that in Him, we find the promise of eternal life and fulfillment of every longing of our hearts.

The journey to wholeness requires us to earnestly study and pray God's Word, believing in its power to manifest God's promises in our lives. As Isaiah 55:11 assures, His Word is potent, accomplishing His desires and prospering in its purpose for us.

As we endeavor to live by God's Word, we step closer to experiencing the richness of His provision—wholeness in every aspect of our being, as echoed in 3 John 1:2. This path of wholeness is not one we walk alone; it is guided by the promise of God's blessings that not only accompany but also overtake us.

Today, let us embrace the courage to pick up our mat—the Word of God—and step into the journey of being made whole. In doing so, we accept Jesus's invitation to a life marked by healing, deliverance, and complete fulfillment in Him. "Be Made Whole."

Week 5 - Journaling Activity:
Stepping Into Wholeness
with God's Word

This journaling activity is crafted to accompany your spiritual journey toward wholeness, as inspired by the devotion "Embarking on the Journey to Wholeness." Through these prompts, you'll explore your own areas of need for God's healing touch, engage deeply with His Word, and document your journey towards the wholeness that Jesus offers.

Day 1: Identifying Areas for Wholeness

- Reflect on the areas of your life where you desire healing and wholeness. Is it physical, emotional, spiritual, or relational? Write them down and openly share your feelings with God in your journal.

Day 2: Understanding Jesus's Invitation

- Meditate on John 5:6. Imagine Jesus asking you, "Will you be made whole?" Journal about your initial reactions and feelings towards this question. Are there any excuses or fears holding you back from saying yes?

Day 3: Lifting Your Mat

- Consider what "picking up your mat" means for you personally. What actions, changes, or steps of faith does this imply in your journey towards wholeness? Write about the specific scriptures that resonate with your current situation.

Day 4: Arming with Scripture

- Search for and write down scriptures that speak to your circumstances. How do these verses challenge or comfort you? Choose one to memorize and reflect on its significance in your journal.

Day 5: The Power of His Word

- Reflect on the promise of Isaiah 55:11. How does understanding that God's Word will not return void change your perspective on praying and declaring scripture over your life?

Day 6: Walking in Wholeness

- Visualize what being made whole looks like in your life. Journal about the changes you anticipate in your physical, emotional, spiritual, and relational health as you apply God's Word daily.

Day 7: Commitment to Study and Prayer

- 2 Timothy 2:15 and 3 John 1:2 highlight the importance of studying God's Word and prospering in all aspects. Write a prayer or commitment to continue seeking wholeness through study and application of the scriptures.

Weekly Reflection:

At the end of the week, review your entries and reflect on the insights gained and the steps taken towards wholeness. Note any scriptures that have become particularly meaningful to you and why. Consider how you can incorporate these reflections into your daily life moving forward.

Continuous Growth:

Keep this journal as a living document of your journey towards wholeness. Return to it often to add new insights, scriptures, and reflections as you continue to grow in your faith and experience the healing power of Jesus's invitation to be made whole.

WEEK 6 - WEEKLY DEVOTION
HOLDING FAST TO YOUR
DIVINE CONFIDENCE

In moments of doubt or hesitation, let's gently remind ourselves to dwell on the unwavering promises of God. Hebrews 10:35-36 offers us a profound encouragement: "So do not throw away your confidence; it will be richly rewarded. You need to persevere so that when you have done the will of God, you will receive what he has promised." (NIV)

What promises from God are you clinging to today? What visions or dreams are you awaiting to see unfold in your life? Consider the patience of Jesus, who, embodying human form, embraced earthly limitations to fulfill the divine plan. His journey on earth—a testament to patience, ending in the ultimate reunion with His Father—teaches us the virtue of waiting with purpose.

1 John 5:14-15 reassures us of the power inherent in approaching God with confidence: "This is the confidence we have in approaching God: that if we ask anything according to his will, he hears us. And if we know that he hears us—whatever we ask—we know that we have what we asked of him." (NIV)

As you stand in faith for your prayers to be answered, begin to declare your desires. Reflect on the narrative of Abraham in Romans Chapter 4, a story of unwavering faith and hope beyond hope, a narrative where the promise of countless descendants was believed even when there seemed no earthly possibility.

Pause for a moment and remind God of His promises concerning your situation. Proclaim them aloud, letting your own ears hear the faith-filled words. Remember, "Faith comes by hearing, and hearing by the word of God" (Romans 10:17, NKJV). Discover your promise in the scriptures and persist in speaking them out loud, nurturing a hope against hope that what has been promised to you will indeed come to fruition.

Hebrews 10:23 encourages us to "hold unswervingly to the hope we profess, for he who promised is faithful." Let this assurance anchor your confidence in God's promises, believing firmly that He rewards those who earnestly seek Him.

Your confidence lies in the understanding that God is capable of exceeding all our expectations, as stated in Ephesians 3:20: "Now to him who is able to do immeasurably more than all we ask or imagine, according to his power that is at work within us." Who does this power work within? You!

Embrace this day with a renewed sense of divine confidence, knowing that your faith and perseverance align you with the extraordinary plans God has for you. Keep your confidence not in the seen, but in the unseen promises of God, and watch as the tapestry of His perfect will unfolds in your life.

Week 6 - Journaling Activity:
Nurturing Your Divine Confidence

This journaling activity is designed to deepen your connection with God's promises, enhancing your understanding and application of the devotion "Holding Fast to Your Divine Confidence." Through introspection, scripture engagement, and proactive faith statements, you'll cultivate a resilient confidence in God's faithfulness.

Day 1: Identifying God's Promises

- Reflect on the promises God has placed in your heart. What are you believing God for? Write these promises down and the scriptures that align with them.

Day 2: Learning from Jesus's Patience

- Meditate on Jesus's journey on earth and His ultimate sacrifice. How does His patience in fulfilling God's will inspire you to persevere in your own waiting period? Journal your thoughts.

Day 3: Confidence in Prayer

- Reflect on 1 John 5:14-15. Write a prayer that expresses your confidence in God's promises, asking according to His will and trusting in His response.

Day 4: Declaring Your Faith

- Inspired by Abraham's story in Romans Chapter 4, write down what "hoping against hope" looks like in your current situation. Declare out loud your faith and hope in God's promises.

Day 5: The Power of God's Word

- Choose a scripture that resonates with your current faith journey. Commit to memorizing it this week. Journal about how this verse speaks to your circumstances and strengthens your confidence.

Day 6: Holding Unswervingly to Hope

- Meditate on Hebrews 10:23. What does it mean for you to "hold unswervingly to the hope" you profess? Journal about the areas in your life where you need to apply unwavering hope and faith.

Day 7: Your Confidence in God's Power

- Contemplate Ephesians 3:20 and the power at work within you. Write a letter to yourself from the future, describing how God did immeasurably more than you asked or imagined.

Weekly Reflection:

At the end of the week, review your journal entries. Reflect on how your understanding and confidence in God's promises have evolved. Identify any changes in your perception or feelings of assurance in God's faithfulness. How can you apply this renewed confidence in your daily life?

Continuous Engagement:

Keep this journal as a living testimony of your faith journey. Return to it in times of doubt, and add new insights, prayers, and declarations as you continue to witness God's faithfulness. Let it be a beacon of divine confidence that guides you through life's uncertainties.

WEEK 7- WEEKLY DEVOTION
WORSHIP

As we enter into a new season, let us experience a breakthrough in our worship. Let's worship Him in the beauty of His holiness. He is our Father, and we honor Him. He is Jehovah Jireh, Shamma, Nissi, Rose of Sharon Lilly of the Valley, and Bright Morning Star. God, who is and is to come. Lion of the tribe of Judah. The everlasting God. He is a friend that sticks closer than a brother. He is El Shaddai, the all-sufficient one. He is the lover of my soul. He is more significant than any problem I face. He is the reigning King. He is the victorious King. He has never lost a battle. He is King of Kings, Lord of Lord, the true and living God. As we worship Him this summer, we will experience a heat wave. A wave of breakthroughs in our lives, our families and friends. We will experience some suddenness. Suddenly, things that we've been praying and fretting about will manifest. We build ourselves up to experience His incredible power as we worship Him.

We are allowing Him access to our spirit, man. We are saying, I surrender to you, Lord. I lay down my agenda and open myself to your agenda for my life. Encouraging ourselves in Him. Before you know it, you will be speaking His promises to yourself. Speak out loud so you can hear what He promises you. Speak health and wholeness. Speak peace and joy. Speak freedom from lack or want. If we would only STOP and worship Him, we would overflow others with emails of testimonials of what God is doing in our lives this summer. God wants you to experience record-breaking temperatures in your personal life so you can walk with Him with full assurance as we enter the seasons of our lives.

Begin today a fresh with worship. Worship brings Him where you are. Worship allows you to experience His greatness. Worship enables the Holy Spirit to hover over you. Worship allows Him to fellowship with you. He wants to share revelation and give you instructions on what to do and how to accomplish what He said. Begin today journaling your experiences with Him. He is longing to share His plans for your life with you. Jeremiah 29:11 says, plans for good and not evil. To bring you to an expected end. Father, thank you for being Jehovah Jireh, the God who provides.

In Jesus Name, Amen.

Week 7 - Journal Activity:
Experiencing Breakthrough
in Worship

Introduction:
As we embrace the warmth of summer and enter a new season, let's deepen our connection with God through a dedicated worship journaling activity. This will be a sacred space to document your reflections, prayers, and the breakthroughs that manifest as you devote yourself to worshipping Him in the beauty of His holiness.

Day 1: Acknowledging His Names

Write down the different names of God mentioned in the devotion (Jehovah Jireh, Shammah, Nissi, etc.). Next to each name, note a personal reflection or a prayer that relates to what each name means to you and how it has impacted your life.

Day 2: Recognizing God's Attributes

Reflect on the attributes of God described in the devotion (e.g., "friend that sticks closer than a brother," "the all-sufficient one"). Choose one attribute and write about a time when you experienced God's presence in this way.

Day 3: Declarations of Faith

Inspired by the devotion, write out loud declarations of faith such as "He is bigger than any problem I face" or "He has never lost a battle." Explain how these declarations help strengthen your faith.

Day 4: Experiencing the Breakthrough

Reflect on any recent breakthroughs in your life, big or small. How do you see God's hand in these situations? Write down these instances and express your gratitude.

Day 5: The Power of Worship

Journal about how worship has transformed your relationship with God. How does worship bring you closer to Him? Describe how you feel when you worship and the changes you notice in your surroundings or circumstances when you worship.

Day 6: Surrender and Submission

Contemplate the idea of surrendering to God's will. What does it mean to lay down your agenda and open yourself to God's agenda for your life? Write a prayer of surrender, asking God to align your desires with His.

Day 7: Listening for God's Voice

How has God spoken to you recently? Record any words, scriptures, impressions, or revelations you believe God has shared with you. How do these insights help guide your decisions and actions?

Weekly Reflection:

At the end of the week, review your journal entries. Reflect on how focusing on each aspect of God's character and your act of worship has impacted your week. Write a summary of how this week's journaling has deepened your understanding and experience of God's greatness.

Closing Prayer:

Father, thank you for being Jehovah Jireh, the God who provides. Thank you for the breakthroughs in worship and for the revelations you have shared. Continue to guide me as I seek to align my life more closely with your will. In Jesus' Name, Amen.

Use this journal as a continual reminder of God's active presence in your life and as a testament to the power of worship to bring about transformation and breakthroughs.

WEEK 8 - WEEKLY DEVOTION
ETERNAL PRESENCE: FROM START TO FINISH, IT'S ALL ABOUT GOD!

The Psalmist passionately proclaims, and it's a truth that resonates deeply within our souls: God is our Refuge, an ever-present help in every twist and turn of life. From the beginning to the middle, and all the way to the end, God's unwavering presence is a source of immeasurable comfort and strength. What a profound comfort it is to know that through every season and stage of our lives, God is steadfastly by our side.

To ensure we're always enveloped in His love and guidance, He blessed us with the Holy Spirit, who resides within us. The Holy Spirit serves as our Comforter, Counselor, Advocate, Intercessor, Guide, Teacher, and so much more—each name a testament to His multifaceted role in our lives. Reflecting on the scripture that declares "the kingdom of God is within you," we're reminded of the profound internal transformation that the Holy Spirit initiates and sustains within us.

When Jesus spoke to the Pharisees in Luke 17:20-21, they were fixated on the signs of an earthly kingdom, failing to recognize that the true transformation Jesus offered was of the heart, not of external circumstances. Similarly, we too can become so engrossed in our challenges and desires for signs that we overlook the miracle of His presence among us.

Today, let's dive deep into meditation and worship with a heart surrendered to His dominion in our lives. The Holy Spirit is eager to transform our hearts, guide our steps, and influence our actions, thoughts, relationships, and families from a place of divine love and wisdom.

Recalling a recent devotional on "Worship," we're reminded of the powerful movements of the Spirit that can be unleashed in such moments—worship is the fertile ground for breakthroughs, the key to unlocking chains, the balm that restores relationships, and the force that sets our spirits free. Worship is not just an act of adoration; it's an activation of the kingdom of God within us, allowing us to connect with our Creator without barriers.

As we continue to navigate the journey of life, let's hold fast to this vibrant truth: In every beginning, throughout every middle, and at every ending, God is profoundly present. By embracing worship and allowing the Holy Spirit to work through us, we celebrate and manifest the eternal kingdom of God in our lives, reflecting His love and light in every moment.

Week 8 - Journal Activity:
Experiencing God's Eternal Presence

This journal activity is inspired by the devotion "Eternal Presence: From Start to Finish, It's All About God!" and is designed to guide you through a reflective exploration of God's omnipresence in every phase of your life. Through thoughtful prompts, you'll discover the profound impact of welcoming the Holy Spirit's transformation within and recognize the power of worship in connecting with the divine.

Day 1: Recognizing God's Presence

- Reflect on a moment from your past where you distinctly felt God's presence. How did this experience affect you? Write about the emotions and revelations that emerged from this encounter.

Day 2: The Role of the Holy Spirit

- Contemplate the various roles the Holy Spirit plays in your life (Comforter, Counselor, Advocate, etc.). Choose one that resonates with you deeply at this moment and journal about how you see this aspect of the Holy Spirit active in your life.

Day 3: The Kingdom of God Within

- Meditate on the idea that "the kingdom of God is within you." What does this mean for your daily life and decisions? How can you more fully embrace this internal transformation?

Day 4: Overcoming Distractions

- Consider a recent time when your focus on problems or desires for signs may have caused you to miss the presence of God. What steps can you take to remain more aware of His presence in all situations?

Day 5: Surrendering to God's Rule

- Write a letter of surrender to God, inviting Him to rule and reign in every area of your life. Include aspects of your life where you especially seek His guidance and transformation.

Day 6: The Power of Worship

- Reflect on a powerful worship experience you've had. How did it ignite the Holy Spirit within you? Describe the breakthroughs, healings, or freedoms you experienced during this time.

Day 7: Worship as a Way of Life

- How can you incorporate worship into your daily routine beyond music or church services? Journal about creative ways to live a life of worship, celebrating the Creator in all you do.

Weekly Reflection:

At the end of the week, review your journal entries and reflect on the insights gained about God's presence throughout every stage of your life. How has your understanding of the Holy Spirit's role and the practice of worship deepened? Identify one action step you can take to foster a deeper connection with God daily.

Continuous Engagement:

Keep this journal as a spiritual diary, returning to these prompts whenever you need a reminder of God's eternal presence in your life. Add new reflections, prayers, and experiences of encountering God to continue cultivating a heart attuned to His omnipresence and love.

WEEK 9 - WEEKLY DEVOTION
EMBRACING OUR HEAVENLY CITIZENSHIP

Philippians 3:20 serves as a gentle, yet profound reminder of our true origin: "But our citizenship is in heaven. And we eagerly await a Savior from there, the Lord Jesus Christ." This passage sparked an incredible revelation in me that I'm eager to share with you.

In the whirlwind of daily life, amidst the flurry of worldly concerns and the well-being of our loved ones, it's all too easy to lose sight of an essential truth. The name of Jesus stands mightily above every trial and tribulation we encounter on this earth. This morning, as I delved into the Scriptures, it dawned on me: our true citizenship, along with all its blessings and privileges, resides in heaven. This perspective shift invites us to lift our gaze, thoughts, and aspirations towards our eternal home, promising that such focus will unleash a torrent of blessings upon us.

You might think, "But I am already living in the blessings." Indeed, you may be experiencing blessings that require certain actions on your part to sustain. However, I'm speaking of blessings so abundant they chase you down, emanating from every direction with the force of a category 5 hurricane— blessings that encompass prosperity in every facet of life: spiritually, emotionally, physically, and financially. This is about stepping into a realm of health, total wellness, and divine revelation so profound that as you engage with the Word and fellowship with the Father, your blessings transform you from merely being blessed to becoming a philanthropist, a financier for the kingdom of God, where scarcity finds no room, and everything in your life operates in a state of overflow.

David proclaimed in Psalm 24:1, "The earth is the Lord's, and everything in it, the world, and all who live in it." Similarly, Apostle Paul affirms in 1 Corinthians 10:26, "The earth is the Lord's, and everything in it." Yes, while the earth belongs to the Lord, it serves as our embassy, not our permanent residence. Our lives ought to be centered on our true home, where we are invited to live without limitations. Here on earth, God has endowed us with "everything we need for a godly life" (2 Peter 1:3), equipping us to live abundantly within this earthly embassy as we await our return to our limitless heavenly home.

Let us, therefore, embrace our heavenly citizenship with full hearts, drawing upon the promises that await us. In our Father's kingdom, we are called to live boundlessly, guided by the knowledge that the Triune God reigns supreme, not only in our heavenly abode but also here, in our earthly embassy. Let's journey forward, claiming the inheritance of our heavenly citizenship, and allow the essence of our divine home to infuse every aspect of our lives here on earth.

Week 9 - Journal Activity: Claiming Your Heavenly Citizenship

This journal activity is designed to accompany the devotion "Embracing Our Heavenly Citizenship," guiding you through a reflective exploration of your spiritual identity and the boundless blessings associated with your citizenship in heaven. Engage with these prompts to deepen your understanding and application of this eternal perspective.

Day 1: Recognizing Your Citizenship

- Reflect on what it means to you that your true citizenship is in heaven. How does this perspective shift affect your view of earthly challenges and blessings?

Day 2: The Name Above All

- Contemplate the power of the name of Jesus in your life. Write about a situation where invoking His name made a difference, and how it reminds you of your heavenly support.

Day 3: Blessings Beyond Measure

- Imagine the blessings that come from focusing on your heavenly citizenship. Describe these "Category 5 hurricane" blessings and how you might start to experience them even now.

Day 4: From Blessed to Blessing

- Reflect on your journey from receiving blessings to becoming a source of blessings (a philanthropist, kingdom financier). What steps can you take to move further along this path?

Day 5: Your Earthly Embassy

- Consider the idea that while the earth is the Lord's, it serves as our embassy, not our permanent home. How does this analogy help you understand your purpose and mission here?

Day 6: Living Without Limits

- Meditate on the limitless life we are invited to live as citizens of heaven. Journal about any limits you've placed on yourself that you need God's help to overcome.

Day 7: Claiming Your Inheritance

- Reflect on the promises of God that pertain to your heavenly citizenship. Write a prayer or declaration claiming these promises and expressing your commitment to live by them.

Weekly Reflection:

At the end of the week, review your responses and consider how the realization of your heavenly citizenship can transform your daily life. Identify any insights gained about living in the overflow of God's blessings and how you can practically apply this understanding to become a more effective ambassador for Christ on earth.

Continuous Growth:

Keep this journal as a living document of your spiritual journey, adding insights, prayers, and reflections on your heavenly citizenship as you grow in your faith. Return to it in moments of doubt or challenge to remind yourself of your true home and the eternal perspective that guides your life.

WEEK 10 - WEEKLY DEVOTION
EMBRACING OUR ROLE AS
COVENANT CREATORS

Diving into Scripture has a way of illuminating truths that flicker like neon signs, and today's flashing message is: Our God is a steadfast covenant keeper. It's a rock-solid guarantee that His promises are not just wishful thinking but certainties that will unfold in our lives and ripple out to touch those we cherish dearly.

Isaiah 59:21 serves up a divine assurance straight from God's heart, "As for me, this is my covenant with them," says the Lord. "My Spirit, who is on you, and my words that I have put in your mouth will not depart from your mouth, or from the mouths of your children, or from the mouths of their descendants from this time on and forever," says the Lord. (NIV). It's like God is saying, "I've got you covered, from this generation to the next!"

Here's a little nudge: let's get chatty with God's Word. Every challenge, every hiccup in life, has got to take a knee when faced with the Word of God. Our Father isn't just a talker; He's a spectacular creator who speaks things into being. And guess what? He's passed that same "create with your words" baton to us. Instead of echoing our worries or gripes, why not declare our desires into existence? He kicked off creation with "Let there be," setting the ultimate example for us.

So, why not sprinkle a little "let there be" magic in our lives too? Let there be laughter ringing through our homes. Let there be a serenity that soothes every frazzled nerve. Let there be love that knows no bounds. And let's not forget about increase – in diving into His Word, in our actions reflecting His love, and in nurturing positive thoughts. As we flip through the Bible, let's start vocalizing the change we yearn to see, wielding our words as tools to sculpt our reality. Your very words have the power to transform the air around you, to expand your influence, to invite abundance into your life. Isaiah 54:2 nudges us to think big and stretch our faith-tents wide – your guardian angels are on standby, just waiting for your "let there be" command.

Philippians 1:6 packs a punch of encouragement, reminding us that the One who ignited this spark within us is committed to fanning it into a blazing fire, all the way till Jesus makes His comeback. You're holding onto a promise here; let's echo it into every corner of our lives.

So, as we journey through each day, let's wear our covenant creator hats with pride, speaking life, joy, and abundance into existence. Remember, in the storybook of our lives, God has penned in a happily ever after with His promises. Let's start living like it, one spoken word at a time.

Week 10 - Journal Activity:
Living as Covenant Creators

This journal activity is inspired by the devotion "Embracing Our Role as Covenant Creators," encouraging you to actively engage with the power of spoken words in shaping your reality, according to God's promises. Through these prompts, explore the depth of God's covenant with you and harness the creative power of your words to align with His will.

Day 1: Understanding Your Covenant

- Reflect on Isaiah 59:21. What does it mean to you that God's Spirit and words will always be with you and your descendants? Write about how this promise shapes your understanding of your identity in God.

Day 2: Speaking Life

- Today, focus on the phrase "Let there be…" Think about areas in your life needing light, joy, peace, or healing. Write down specific "Let there be…" declarations for these areas.

Day 3: The Power of Creation

- Consider how God spoke the world into existence and has given you the power to speak your world into existence as well. Journal about what it means to you to have this creative power through your words.

Day 4: Increasing Your Faith-Tent

- Meditate on Isaiah 54:2. What does "enlarging the place of your tent" look like in your spiritual life, relationships, career, or ministry? Envision and write about expanding beyond your current borders.

Day 5: Your Angelic Assignments

- Reflect on the idea that your words give assignments to angels. What messages or missions do you want to send to your angels today? Write them as clear commands or prayers.

Day 6: The Assurance of Completion

- Ponder Philippians 1:6. How does the assurance that God will complete the good work He started in you affect your faith and actions? Write a prayer or affirmation of trust in God's faithfulness to complete His work in you.

Day 7: Speaking Promises Aloud

- Choose a promise from Scripture that resonates with your current season or situation. Write it out and then spend time speaking it aloud, declaring it over your life. Reflect on the power of hearing God's promises in your own voice.

Weekly Reflection:

At the end of the week, review your journal entries and reflect on how this practice of speaking God's promises has influenced your mindset, faith, and circumstances. Note any changes you've observed in yourself or your environment and how you can continue to implement this practice in your daily life.

Continuous Engagement:

Keep this journal as a testament to the power of your words aligned with God's Word. Return to it whenever you need a reminder of your role as a covenant creator, and continue to add new insights, declarations, and reflections on the promises of God as you journey through life.

WEEK 11 - WEEKLY DEVOTION
EMBRACING OUR IMPERFECTIONS WITH GRACE

I t's a funny thing about us humans; we're quick to spot a speck in someone else's eye while overlooking the log in our own. We find ourselves at times, saying, "That's it! I'm done with that person!" over hurts and offenses, forgetting how wonderfully flawed we ourselves are. During a chat with a friend, the topic of our imperfections popped up, and I felt a nudge from the Holy Spirit. It was as if He was gently chuckling and pointing out, "Notice how easily you spot flaws in others, yet conveniently forget your own?"

That moment of divine humor made me pause. The Holy Spirit, ever the gentle guide, suggested a different approach: What if, instead of assigning blame, we tried understanding where the other person is coming from? Their concerns and feelings are as real to them as ours are to us. He nudged me towards the idea of returning to the "Potter's House"—to lay my own flawed self upon God's refining wheel. There, in the hands of the ultimate Craftsman, my own imperfections could be smoothed over, preparing me to respond with grace and empathy.

This revelation was a reminder that we're all navigating this life as wonderfully imperfect beings. We might say, "I left that church because they hurt me," placing the blame on the collective when, in reality, it was our expectations of flawed individuals that led to disappointment. It's crucial to remember that everyone—from church leaders to coworkers, neighbors, and friends—is doing their best within the bounds of their human imperfections.

As I reflected on this, the Holy Spirit whispered a reminder of the "Potter's House," where judgment is set aside in favor of understanding and growth. It brought to mind Matthew 7:3, which speaks volumes about our tendency to judge others without recognizing our own imperfections. Yes, it's hilariously true—I'm flawed, and so are you.

Committing to letting the Potter work on our imperfections means acknowledging our need for regular 'maintenance' by the Holy Spirit. Our founding Pastor Tony Ashmore once said, "We all leak." It's a humorous yet profound reminder that we are all leaking, flawed individuals in need of the Holy Spirit's touch.

So, let's agree to approach each other with more grace and understanding, recognizing that we are all works in progress, continually being shaped by the Potter's hands. By embracing our imperfections and allowing the Holy Spirit to refine us, we can foster a community of compassion, patience, and love— leaks and all.

Week 11 - Journal Activity:
Navigating Our Flaws with Grace

This journal activity is inspired by the devotion "Embracing Our Imperfections with Grace," offering you a daily guide to introspection and growth in understanding both your imperfections and those of others. Each day, you'll have the opportunity to reflect, listen, and allow the Holy Spirit to work through your life, smoothing out the rough edges and teaching you to extend grace as freely as you hope to receive it.

Day 1: Recognizing Your Flaws

- Reflect on a recent situation where you were quick to judge or dismiss someone. What flaws in yourself might have influenced your reaction? Write about these imperfections and how acknowledging them makes you feel.

Day 2: The Perspective of Others

- Think of a time when someone misunderstood you or didn't see your point of view. Write about how it made you feel and how this experience can help you offer more understanding to others.

Day 3: Listening with the Heart

- Today, focus on listening more intently to those around you. At the end of the day, journal about the experience. Did you learn anything new about someone by listening more deeply?

Day 4: Visiting the Potter's House

- Imagine yourself in the Potter's House, being reshaped by God's hands. What specific flaw or imperfection would you like Him to smooth out? Write a prayer inviting the Holy Spirit to work on this aspect of your character.

Day 5: The Gift of Empathy

- Reflect on a relationship that might benefit from more empathy on your part. Journal about how you can apply understanding and patience to this relationship, inspired by your own journey of being refined.

Day 6: Embracing Imperfections in Others

- Think of someone in your life who is "flawed" in a way that challenges you. Write about their positive qualities and how you can look past their imperfections to see the beauty in their uniqueness.

Day 7: Offering and Receiving Grace

- Reflect on the grace God offers you despite your imperfections. How can you extend the same grace to others? Write about specific ways you can practice this in your daily interactions.

Weekly Reflection:

At the end of the week, review your journal entries and reflect on the lessons learned about yourself and others. How has this week's focus on navigating flaws with grace changed your interactions or your perceptions? Identify one action step you can take to continue growing in grace and empathy.

Continuous Growth:

Keep this journal as a testament to your journey of embracing imperfections with grace. Add new insights, prayers, and reflections as you continue to navigate the beautifully flawed human experience, guided by the Holy Spirit's gentle refinement.

WEEK 12 - WEEKLY DEVOTION
HE KNOWS ME BY NAME: A REMINDER OF DIVINE INTIMACY

Isn't it a bit awkward when you bump into someone whose name just slips through the cracks of your memory? Yet, in the vast expanse of the universe, our Heavenly Father not only remembers our names but knows us more deeply than we know ourselves. David, in his poetic masterpiece Psalm 139, unravels this profound truth about God's intimate knowledge of us. Let's soak in the essence of verses 1 through 4: "O Lord, you have searched me and known me! You know when I sit down and when I rise up; you discern my thoughts from afar. You search out my path and my lying down and are acquainted with all my ways. Even before a word is on my tongue, behold, O Lord, you know it altogether." (ESV)

Reflecting on this, I couldn't help but smile as the Holy Spirit whispered a reminder, "He knows your name, and did you remember, the same Spirit that resurrected Jesus lives in you? Do you grasp that? The divine power you carry hinges on your faith and belief in the miracle-working power dwelling within you." This got me thinking about Ephesians 3:20, "Now to him who is able to do immeasurably more than all we ask or imagine, according to his power that is at work within us." (NIV)

Yes, within each of us is a reservoir of resurrection power, waiting to be unleashed not just for our benefit but to transform the lives around us—our families, friends, neighbors, and even the strangers we encounter. Psalm 139 doesn't just highlight God's omniscience; it's a love letter, revealing His desire for closeness, His eagerness to engage with us, and His patience as He waits for us to seek His embrace.

So, the next time you're scrambling to recall someone's name, remember this: While our minds may sometimes fail us, there's a God who formed us, knows us intimately, and calls us by name. And if the conversation permits, share this beautiful truth: "I might momentarily forget a name, but there's a God who knew you, named you, and loves you, long before we ever met." Amen!

Week 12 - Journal Activity:
Discovering Our Name
in God's Heart

Inspired by the devotion "He Knows Me by Name: A Reminder of Divine Intimacy," this journal activity invites you to explore the depth of God's intimate knowledge of you and the resurrection power that resides within. Through thoughtful reflection and creative expression, you'll deepen your understanding of your identity in God and how His eternal presence shapes your life.

Day 1: Known by God

- Reflect on what it means to you personally that God knows everything about you, including your name. Write a letter to God expressing your thoughts and feelings about His intimate knowledge of you.

Day 2: Resurrection Power Within

- Meditate on the truth that the same Spirit that raised Jesus from the dead dwells in you (Romans 8:11). Journal about what resurrection power means in your daily life. How does it change the way you view challenges or opportunities?

Day 3: The Intimacy of Psalm 139

- Read Psalm 139:1-4 again slowly. Pick one verse that resonates with you the most today. Write it down and then journal about why it stands out to you and how it speaks to your current situation or feelings.

Day 4: Exercising Faith

- Ephesians 3:20 speaks of God's ability to do immeasurably more than we ask or imagine. Reflect on an area of your life where you need to exercise more faith. Write a prayer asking God to help you trust in His immeasurable power at work within you.

Day 5: Your Name in His Hands

- Imagine God speaking your name. What emotions or thoughts does this evoke in you? Journal about the significance of being named and known by God, and how this impacts your sense of identity and purpose.

Day 6: Transforming Power

- Consider how the resurrection power within you can impact the lives of others. Journal about one specific way you can use your God-given power to make a positive change in someone else's life this week.

Day 7: Eternal Fellowship

- Psalm 139 reveals God's desire for closeness with us. Reflect on how you can respond to God's invitation for deeper fellowship. Journal about one step you can take this week to draw nearer to Him in your daily routine.

Weekly Reflection:

At the end of the week, review your journal entries. Reflect on the insights gained about God's intimate knowledge of you and the power He has placed within you. Identify any patterns or recurring themes that emerged during your reflections. Consider how you can incorporate these insights into your ongoing walk with God.

Continuous Engagement:

Keep this journal as a living document of your spiritual journey. Return to it in moments of doubt or when you need a reminder of your identity in Christ. Continue to add new reflections, prayers, and experiences as you grow in your understanding of God's intimate knowledge of you and the resurrection power at work within you.

WEEK 13 - WEEKLY DEVOITION
A GENTLE NUDGE FROM EZEKIEL:
HONORING HIS NAME

On a brisk morning, January 5, 2017, with my coffee in one hand and the Bible in the other, I dove into my SOAP reading which landed me in Ezekiel 36. Verse 22 struck a chord, and it felt as though the Holy Spirit leaned in with a knowing smile, whispering, "Sometimes, you know, you take my grace for granted." Ezekiel 36:22 spells it out: "Therefore say to the Israelites, 'This is what the Sovereign LORD says: It is not for your sake, people of Israel, that I am going to do these things, but for the sake of my holy name, which you have profaned among the nations where you have gone.'" (NIV)

As I chewed on that verse, a montage of my own not-so-glorious moments—thoughts, actions, and all—played in my mind. It was both a humbling and a face-palm moment to realize that God had been moving mountains for me, not because I was the poster child for perfection, but for the sake of His glorious Name and His steadfast Word.

With the dawn of 2017 upon us, I found myself musing over a new resolution: to make choices rooted in His Word and aimed at honoring His Name. After all, we're talking about a God who's got a track record of doing the extraordinary in our lives. Wrapping up my time in divine conversation, I offered up a heartfelt prayer: "Lord, as I soak in Your Word and enjoy this divine tête-à-tête, help me to be a guardian of Your Name and

Your Word. Let it not be my blunders but my faithfulness that prompts You to act on my behalf. I'm laying it all down at Your feet today—my thoughts, my feelings, and my actions. I'm all in for a now 2024 filled with blessings rooted in our loyalty to You. In Jesus' Name, Amen."

So here's to a year of living wisely, with a dash of humor and a heap of warmth, all while keeping the honor of His Name at the forefront of everything we do.

Week 13 - Journaling Activity: Honoring His Name in Our Daily Walk

This journaling activity is inspired by the devotion "A Gentle Nudge from Ezekiel: Honoring His Name," encouraging you to reflect on the importance of living a life that honors God's name through your actions, thoughts, and decisions. Each day, you're invited to explore different aspects of your life where you can more intentionally reflect God's grace and maintain the integrity of His holy name.

Day 1: Reflecting on Grace

- Reflect on a recent moment when you became aware of taking God's grace for granted. Write about this experience and how you felt upon this realization.

Day 2: Actions and Thoughts

- Consider the actions or thoughts from the past week that may not have honored God's name. Journal about these instances and what you could do differently moving forward.

Day 3: For His Name's Sake

- Meditate on the idea that God acts for the sake of His holy name. Write about what this tells you about God's character and how it affects your understanding of your relationship with Him.

Day 4: Decision Making

- Think about a decision you need to make soon. Journal about how you can ensure this decision is based on His Word and honors His name.

Day 5: A Prayer of Surrender

- Inspired by the devotion's prayer, write your own prayer of surrender. Offer your thoughts, emotions, and deeds to God, asking for His guidance to live a life that glorifies His name.

Day 6: Faithfulness Over Foolishness

- Reflect on what it means to have God move on your behalf because of faithfulness rather than foolishness. Journal about areas in your life where you need to grow in faithfulness.

Day 7: Setting Intentions for Faithfulness

- As you consider the year ahead, write down specific intentions or resolutions that focus on protecting God's name through your faithfulness. How will you implement these in your daily life?

Weekly Reflection:

At the end of the week, review your journal entries and reflect on the insights gained about honoring God's name through your life. Identify one or two key areas where you feel called to make changes or improvements. Commit to taking actionable steps towards these goals in the coming weeks.

Continuous Engagement:

Keep this journal as a living document of your journey towards honoring God's name in all you do. Return to it periodically to add new reflections, prayers, and experiences that showcase your commitment to living a life that reflects the holiness and grace of God's name.

WEEK 14 - WEEKLY DEVOTION
HOPE AGAINST HOPE

The other day, while reading Paul's letter to Philemon, I felt as if the Holy Spirit granted me a deeper understanding of Paul's letters to the churches, individuals, and people to whom he shared the gospel of Jesus Christ's cross. I noticed that Paul always infused his letters with words of encouragement, even when he needed to offer rebuke. However, in the Book of Philemon, his writing adopts a tone of seeking forgiveness and reconciliation for one of his spiritual sons.

After his warm introductions, he immediately launches into a prayer of thanksgiving for them. He expresses gratitude for their faithfulness to their fellow co-workers in the gospel and their partnership with him. Then, he delicately broaches the subject of Onesimus, requesting that they welcome back into their fellowship someone who had been imprisoned alongside him. He speaks of the deep pain in his heart, yet he acknowledges the necessity of sending Onesimus back.

As we embark on our day, let's pause for some reflection on how we navigate our relationships, especially those that may benefit from healing, mending, or forgiveness. Like Paul, who demonstrated grace in encouraging reconciliation even from afar, we are invited to become conduits of healing and unity.

Week 14 - Journaling Activity:
Nurturing Reconciliation and Hope

Inspired by the devotion "Hope Against Hope," this journaling activity invites you to explore the themes of forgiveness, reconciliation, and the transformative power of extending grace, as exemplified in Paul's letter to Philemon. Through thoughtful reflection and personal introspection, you'll discover ways to apply these timeless principles in your own life.

Day 1: Understanding Forgiveness

- Reflect on a situation where you found it challenging to offer forgiveness. Write about the emotions involved and what makes forgiveness difficult in this scenario.

Day 2: The Power of Encouragement

- Think of a time when someone's encouragement made a significant difference in your life, especially during a period of correction or rebuke. Journal about the impact of that encouragement and how it helped you grow.

Day 3: Paul's Approach to Reconciliation

- Consider Paul's gentle yet direct approach in seeking Onesimus's reconciliation with Philemon. Write about how you can adopt a similar approach in mending a strained relationship in your life.

Day 4: Reflection on Second Chances

- Onesimus's story is one of transformation and second chances. Reflect on an instance where you were given a second chance. How did it change your perspective or direction?

Day 5: The Role of Spiritual Guidance

- Paul played a crucial role in guiding both Philemon and Onesimus towards reconciliation. Journal about someone who has been a spiritual guide in your life and the lessons you've learned from them.

Day 6: Taking Steps Towards Reconciliation

- Identify a relationship in your life that could benefit from reconciliation. List practical steps you can take to initiate healing, inspired by Paul's example of advocacy and love.

Day 7: A Prayer for Hope and Renewal

- Write a prayer asking for the strength to hope against hope in challenging situations, to forgive as you have been forgiven, and for the courage to pursue reconciliation where it is needed.

Weekly Reflection:

At the end of the week, review your journal entries and reflect on the insights you've gained about forgiveness, encouragement, and reconciliation. Consider how you can continue to cultivate these qualities in your life. Identify one action you can take in the coming week to apply what you've learned, whether it's reaching out to mend a relationship, offering forgiveness, or simply extending grace to yourself or others.

Continuous Engagement:

Keep this journal as a resource to revisit when you face challenges in relationships or need encouragement to extend forgiveness and hope. Add to it as you encounter new situations that call for the wisdom and principles reflected in Paul's letter to Philemon, allowing your journey of reconciliation and healing to evolve and deepen.

WEEK 15 -WEEKLY DEVOTION
WALKING TOGETHER: A MESSAGE
OF COMFORT AND GUIDANCE

Hello, Blessed Companions! As I sat down to craft our devotional message for the week, a gentle nudge from the Holy Spirit redirected me towards sharing one that particularly resonated with me recently. My hope is that it offers you as much solace and encouragement as it did for me.

I AM WITH YOU ON THIS JOURNEY

"Trust in the Lord with all your heart and lean not on your own understanding; in all your ways submit to him, and he will make your paths straight" (Proverbs 3:5-6, NIV).

My child, you are a masterpiece crafted with the utmost care. In envisioning you, I thought of your laughter, your thoughts, the unique timbre of your voice. I shaped you with a specific purpose, blessing you with talents that are singularly yours—gifts that are, in themselves, a reflection of my love for you.

You weren't created to be weighed down by the world's demands or to chase after fleeting accolades. You are not defined by the burdens you bear or the exhaustion that tugs at your spirit.

I know the journey with Me may sometimes feel daunting; the path ahead might seem endlessly winding. But remember, I am by your side, every step of the way.

It's time to venture into the unknown, even when the next step isn't visible. Extend your hand; I am eager to grasp it and guide you. Allow me to lift the weight from your shoulders, to ease the load you've been carrying.

Visualize my hands gently removing the heaviness from you. Can you feel the liberation as your chains fall away? Can you sense the unseen forces at work, even if they escape your sight?

I champion your cause, my beloved. I wouldn't send you forth into a wilderness where I won't accompany you. Follow me where my presence leads. Although the path ahead might not be visible, I can see it clearly—I pave the way and ensure it's safe for you.

Follow my lead, my precious one. I am intimately familiar with the journey that lies before you. Every crossroad, every decision point, is an opportunity to seek my direction. Inquire where I am leading, and trust in the assurance that I, the one who lovingly crafted you, am guiding you every step of the way, knowing the intricacies of the path that's just right for you.

In this shared journey of faith, may we always remember the closeness and guiding hand of our Creator, embracing the comfort and direction He so generously provides.

Week 15 - Journaling Activity:
Embracing the Journey with God

Inspired by the devotion "Walking Together: A Message of Comfort and Guidance," this journaling activity invites you to reflect on the presence and guidance of God in your life's journey. Through introspection and prayerful writing, explore how you can more deeply trust in God's path for you, recognizing His hand in every step and decision.

Day 1: Recognizing God's Masterpiece

- Reflect on the idea that you were created intentionally, with unique gifts and a purpose. Write about the qualities or talents you possess that you believe are God-given gifts. How can you use these gifts to honor God?

Day 2: Letting Go of Worldly Pressures

- Consider the pressures and expectations you feel from the world around you. Journal about how these have affected your walk with God and how you can release them to focus more on what God desires for you.

Day 3: Feeling God's Presence on the Journey

- Recall a time when you felt God's presence guiding you through a difficult or uncertain part of your life. Write about this experience and how it strengthened your trust in God.

Day 4: Holding Hands with God

- Imagine extending your hand to God, allowing Him to lead you into the unknown. What fears or hesitations do you need to overcome to take His hand more confidently? Write a prayer asking for courage and faith to trust in His guidance.

Day 5: Visualizing God's Burden-Lifting Hands

- Reflect on the burdens you're currently carrying. How do they weigh you down? Visualize God lifting these from your shoulders and write about the relief and freedom this brings.

Day 6: Following God's Lead

- Think about the choices and decisions before you. What steps can you take to ensure you're following God's lead? Write about how you can incorporate seeking God's presence and guidance into your decision-making process.

Day 7: Trusting in the Unseen

- Meditate on the times you've had to trust in God's plan without seeing the whole path. Journal about what trusting in the unseen looks like for you moving forward. How can you cultivate a deeper trust in God's unseen guidance?

Weekly Reflection:

At the end of the week, review your journal entries. Reflect on the insights you've gained about God's intimate knowledge of you, His desire to guide you, and your ability to trust in His journey for you. Identify one action you can take in the coming week to more closely align your path with God's guidance and presence.

Continuous Engagement:

Keep this journal as a reminder of your ongoing journey with God. Return to these prompts whenever you need reassurance of God's guiding presence in your life. Add new reflections, prayers, and experiences as you continue to walk hand in hand with God, embracing each step of the journey with faith and trust.

WEEK 16 - WEEKLY DEVOTION
IF GOD IS FOR ME, WHO
DARES STAND AGAINST?

"What, then, shall we say in response to these things? If God is for us, who can be against us?" Romans 8:31 beams like a lighthouse through the fog of our daily trials and tribulations, doesn't it? Imagine moving through each day with the serene confidence of a lion who knows its home is secure, filled with a quiet heart that whispers, "God's got this."

Think about it: We're the VIPs of Creation, handcrafted for greatness, designated as God's "Masterpiece" to radiate His glory like a lighthouse on a cliff. Let this truth sink in—God is cheering for you. He designed you for companionship with Him, to fill your soul with a contentment that only the Creator can offer. Yes, in every high and every low, God stands with you.

Consider yourself the favored sheep under the watchful eye of the Good Shepherd, marked as His own. How could He not champion your cause? When life throws curveballs, wear the banner *"GOD IS FOR ME"* like a superhero's cape. Our God reigns supreme, unmatched in power, overflowing with grace. He assures us in Isaiah 54:17 that no weapon fashioned against us will succeed. And just in case we need a reminder of His absolute sovereignty, He adds in verse 56, *"See, it is I who created the blacksmith..."* He's basically saying, "I'm the boss of everything— even the stuff that tries to trip you up."

Just as He nurtures the flowers with rain and morning dew, God is meticulously tending to every detail of your life. He tells us in Matthew 6:25-34 that we outshine the lilies and sparrows in value. So, I'm nudging you today to boldly proclaim, "God Is For Me," and let that declaration transform your surroundings—the kitchen, the office, the daily commute, and especially, the way you perceive the Almighty, who takes delight in you.

So, go on, declare it loud enough for the heavens and your coffee cup to hear: "God Is For Me." Let this affirmation shift the atmosphere around you, turning your space into a sanctuary of faith and your mindset into a fortress of joy and confidence. Dive into Romans 8 and wear that assurance like a crown, knowing well that when God is your advocate, victory is not just an option; it's a guarantee.

Week 16 - Journal Activity:
Embracing the Assurance
"God Is For Me"

This journaling activity, inspired by the devotion "If God Is For Me, Who Dares Stand Against?", is designed to deepen your understanding and conviction of God's unwavering support for you. Through reflection and creative expression, you'll explore the significance of this divine backing in your everyday life.

Day 1: Understanding God's Support

- Reflect on the initial reaction you have to the statement, "God is for me." Write about a recent situation where you felt God's support. How did it change the outcome or your perspective on the situation?

Day 2: God's Masterpiece

- Contemplate what it means to be God's "Masterpiece." Journal about the gifts and talents you believe God has bestowed upon you. How can you use these gifts to reflect God's glory in your daily life?

Day 3: Bold Declarations

- Challenge yourself to declare "God Is For Me" at three different times today when you feel doubt, fear, or anxiety. At the end of the day, journal about your experiences and any shifts in your mood or circumstances.

Day 4: No Weapon Formed Shall Prosper

- Reflect on Isaiah 54:17, focusing on God's sovereignty over all creation, including your challenges. Write about a "weapon" formed against you and how you see God's promise playing out in disarming this weapon.

Day 5: More Valuable Than Sparrows

- Meditate on Matthew 6:25-34, focusing on the part where Jesus speaks about our value over sparrows. Journal about what this passage reveals about God's care for you and how it reassures your worth to Him.

Day 6: The Atmosphere of Faith

- Consider how declaring "God Is For Me" can change the atmosphere of your home, workplace, or personal space. Plan and journal about specific ways you can manifest this atmosphere of faith in your surroundings.

Day 7: A Prayer of Confidence

- Write a prayer that encapsulates your journey through this week, highlighting your newfound or deepened understanding of God being for you. Ask for continued courage to declare this truth in every aspect of your life.

Weekly Reflection:

At the end of the week, review your journal entries. Reflect on how the daily practice of recognizing and declaring "God Is For Me" has impacted your faith, attitude, and actions. Identify one insight or practice you want to carry forward and integrate more deeply into your life.

Continuous Engagement:

Keep this journal as a testament to your growth in faith and confidence in God's support. Return to it whenever you need a reminder of God's backing or when you encounter new challenges. Continue to add reflections, declarations, and prayers as you walk in the assurance that God is always for you.

WEEK 17 - WEEKLY DEVOTION
FROM START TO FINISH: IT'S ALWAYS BEEN GOD

The Psalmist sings it like a catchy tune that gets stuck in your head—God is our Refuge, our constant companion through thick and thin. Picture this: In the beginning, God was the opening act; in the messy middle, He was the plot twist we all cheered for; and you can bet your last chocolate chip cookie, He'll be there for the grand finale. Isn't it heartwarming to know that through every high and low of our lives, God's presence is a given?

But wait, there's more! God didn't just promise to stick around; He went ahead and made Himself at home within us by sending the Holy Spirit. Talk about a divine houseguest! The Holy Spirit isn't just hanging out sipping tea; He's our go-to guy—Comforter, Counselor, Advocate, Intercessor, Guide, Teacher, and yes, even our Witness. These are just a few of His titles, and honestly, they barely scratch the surface. Jesus reminded us that "the kingdom of God is within you," sparking a light that even the Pharisees, with their VIP seats, missed while they were busy waiting for an earthly spectacle.

How often do we find ourselves in the Pharisees' sandals, squinting for signs and wonders while missing the miracle of His presence in the mundane? Today, let's shift gears and tune into His frequency, surrendering to His governance in every aspect of our lives. The Holy Spirit is itching to give our hearts a total makeover, transforming us from the inside out. When we let the kingdom of God take the driver's seat, it not only reroutes our personal journey but also sends ripples through our interactions, thoughts, and even our family dynamics.

Remember that soul-stirring devotional on "Worship" from a few weeks back? It turns out, worship is the spark that lights the fire of the Holy Spirit within us. It's in these moments of unfiltered praise that we find breakthroughs budding, chains disintegrating, and relationships mending. Worship liberates us, allowing us to engage with the Creator in the most authentic and uninhibited way possible.

So, as we navigate the ebbs and flows of life, let's keep this anthem in our hearts: In the beginning, God. In the middle, God. And when the curtain falls at the end, God. With every beat of our worship, let's fan the flames of the kingdom within, celebrating the eternal presence that guides, protects, and loves us—from start to finish.

Week 17 - Journaling Activity:
Recognizing God's Presence
From Start to Finish

Inspired by the devotion "From Start to Finish: It's Always Been God," this journaling activity is designed to deepen your awareness of God's enduring presence in your life and the transformative power of the Holy Spirit and worship. Each day, you'll explore different aspects of God's companionship, the Holy Spirit's roles, and the impact of worship on your spiritual journey.

Day 1: Acknowledging God's Presence

- Reflect on a moment from the beginning of a significant journey in your life. How did you see God present in that beginning? Write about the feelings and thoughts you had, knowing God was with you from the start.

Day 2: The Holy Spirit's Roles

- Choose one of the roles of the Holy Spirit mentioned (Comforter, Counselor, Advocate, Intercessor, Guide, Teacher, Witness) that you feel you need most right now. Journal about a current situation where this role of the Holy Spirit can make a difference.

Day 3: Missing the Miraculous

- Think about a time when, like the Pharisees, you might have been waiting for a sign from God and missed the miracles happening in the mundane. Write about what you learned from this reflection.

Day 4: Surrender to His Rule

- What does surrendering to God's rule and reign in your life look like practically? Journal about one area of your life where you need to surrender more fully to God and invite the Holy Spirit to transform you.

Day 5: The Impact of Worship

- Recall a profound worship experience. Describe how it felt and the changes it ignited within you. How did this experience help you connect more deeply with God?

Day 6: The Kingdom Within

- Meditate on the idea that "the kingdom of God is within you." Journal about how this truth influences your daily actions, thoughts, and relationships.

Day 7: God's Everlasting Presence

- Reflect on the assurance that God is with you from the beginning to the end of your life's story. Write a prayer of gratitude for His constant presence and the promise that He will be with you through every chapter of your life.

Weekly Reflection:

At the end of the week, review your journal entries. Reflect on how recognizing God's presence from start to finish, understanding the Holy Spirit's role in your life, and engaging in worship can transform your spiritual journey. Identify one insight or action step that you can take to cultivate a deeper relationship with God in the coming weeks.

Continuous Engagement:

Keep this journal as a spiritual diary, documenting your ongoing encounters with God's presence, the Holy Spirit's guidance, and moments of worship. Return to it whenever you need a reminder of God's faithfulness and love throughout every phase of your life. Continue to add new reflections, prayers, and revelations as you walk with God, from start to finish.

WEEK 18 - WEEKLY DEVOTION
CALLING ALL ANGELS: A LESSON
FROM HEZEKIAH'S PLAYBOOK

Dive into II Kings, Chapters 18 & 19, for a bit of ancient drama that rivals any modern-day thriller. Picture this: King Hezekiah of Jerusalem is facing the ultimate bully, the King of Assyria, who's on a winning streak, gobbling up cities like they're going out of style. Initially, Hezekiah tries to buy peace, emptying the temple treasury in a move that probably had the celestial beings face-palming. But when the Assyrian king sends a "We're still coming to crush you" memo, Hezekiah switches tactics, trading his royal robes for sackcloth and seeking divine counsel.

Fast forward, and we find Hezekiah spreading a threatening letter before the Lord in the temple, essentially saying, "You're the real MVP, God. Show them who's boss." Spoiler alert: God sends an angelic hitman who takes out 185,000 Assyrian soldiers overnight. Jerusalem's scoreboard lights up without the home team lifting a finger.

So, when the storms of life have you feeling like Hezekiah with his back against the wall, what's your game plan? Do you hit speed dial and rally the prayer warriors, or do you try to negotiate your way out, hoping to appease the onslaught? Maybe it's time we take a page out of Hezekiah's playbook: Pray first, lay it all out before the Lord, and let Him dispatch our angels on assignment.

Facing adversity? Here's a thought: Instead of broadcasting our woes from the rooftops, why not hit our knees, confess our vulnerabilities, and seek the victory stance in prayer first? Imagine the heavenly dispatch center, angels leaning over the edge of their seats, waiting for the go-ahead to swoop in on our behalf. And they're not just any angels; they're our personal celestial bodyguards, ready to defend, protect, and claim victory.

Take solace in Psalm 91, and don't just read it—personalize it. Write your name into those promises because, let's be honest, they're tailor-made for you. God's assurances are a resounding "Yes!" and "Amen!"

Consider this a gentle nudge, wrapped in humor and warmth, from someone who's seen a few gusts of adversity blow through. Seeking God first and activating your angelic support squad can flip the script on any situation. It might not always feel like a win in the moment, but upon reflection, you'll see God's handiwork clear as day.

So, fellow travelers, let's get our angels on assignment. Victory isn't just possible—it's promised. And remember, through every high and low, in the beginning, middle, and end, it's always been God steering the ship. Be encouraged, and let's make those heavenly phone lines buzz with prayers that set our angels into action.

Week 18 - Journaling Activity: Activating Your Angelic Support Squad

Inspired by the devotion "Calling All Angels: A Lesson from Hezekiah's Playbook," this journaling activity invites you to explore the themes of divine intervention, prayerful surrender, and the realization that, in every challenge, victory is woven into the fabric of our faith. Each prompt encourages a deeper connection with God, acknowledging His sovereignty, and recognizing the angelic forces at our disposal.

Day 1: Identifying Your Assyria

- Reflect on a current situation in your life that feels like an advancing Assyrian army—overwhelming and seemingly invincible. Write about this challenge and how it affects you.

Day 2: Your First Response

- Think about your initial reactions to facing adversity. Are you more inclined to seek human solutions or divine intervention? Journal about your typical go-to responses and how they have served you.

Day 3: Laying It Before the Lord

- Inspired by King Hezekiah's act of spreading the threatening letter before God, take a moment to write down the details of your current challenge. Imagine physically laying it out before God in prayer, seeking His guidance.

Day 4: Calling on Your Angelic Squad

- Write a prayer or declaration inviting God to dispatch your angelic support squad. Express your trust in His divine intervention and your readiness to witness His power in action.

Day 5: Personalizing Psalm 91

- Open to Psalm 91 and read it through once. Then, rewrite parts of it, inserting your name and specific circumstances to personalize God's promises of protection and deliverance.

Day 6: Reflection on God's Faithfulness

- Reflect on past instances where you've seen God's hand at work in your life, especially in times of difficulty. Journal about these moments and how they bolster your faith now.

Day 7: Victory in Hindsight

- Consider a past adversity that, in the moment, felt insurmountable but now, in hindsight, you can see led to unexpected growth or blessings. Write about this experience and the role of faith and perhaps unseen celestial intervention.

Weekly Reflection:

At the end of the week, review your journal entries and consider the insights gained about trusting in God's power, the importance of prayerful surrender, and the reality of angelic support. How has this week's focus shifted your perspective on facing challenges? Identify one actionable step you can take to incorporate this trust and surrender into your daily walk with God.

Continuous Engagement:

Keep this journal as a testament to your journey of faith and the lessons learned along the way. Return to these prompts whenever you face new challenges or when you need a reminder of God's unfailing support and the angelic forces ready to act on your behalf. Continue to document your prayers, victories, and reflections, building a legacy of faith for years to come.

WEEK 19 - WEEKLY DEVOTION
EXPLORING THE MANY FACETS OF GOD

I magine God as a gemstone, sparkling with countless facets, each reflecting a different aspect of His divine nature. Yes, I'm talking about the God who's got more skills than a Swiss Army knife, more roles than a seasoned actor, yet, amidst His cosmic versatility, He remains as constant as the North Star. "For I, the Lord, do not change..." Malachi 3:10 whispers, reminding us of His steadfast presence through every twist and turn of life.

Multifaceted isn't just a fancy word you throw around at parties; it perfectly encapsulates the essence of God. He wears many hats, plays numerous roles, all while being the unchanging anchor in our lives. Let's take a stroll through the gallery of His divine dimensions:

- Jehovah-Shalom: Our personal peace negotiator, offering tranquility in life's chaos.
- Jehovah-Jireh: The provider of our needs, from daily bread to unforeseen blessings.
- Jehovah-Rophe: Our divine healer, stitching up wounds both visible and unseen.
- Absolute: The unparalleled one, as Psalms 86:8-10 sets Him apart from the crowd.
- Deliverer: Our superhero, swooping in to save the day, as professed in Psalm 34:4.
- Dependable: The one who never breaks a promise, making Numbers 23:19 our go-to for reassurance.

- Unchanging: The eternal foundation, unshaken and steadfast, as celebrated in Hebrews 1:10-12.

These are just a few highlights from His impressive portfolio. When I pause to ponder His magnificence, I'm awestruck by the vastness of His capabilities coupled with His unwavering consistency. What a remarkable God we are privileged to know! One who adapts to our every need, yet remains an unchanging beacon of love and mercy through His multifaceted characteristics.

Now, it's your turn to explore our Multifaceted God. Reflect on how you've experienced His dynamic presence and how He's shown Himself mighty in your life. Kickstart your own journaling adventure to dive deep into the fullness of His nature. Journaling not only captures His words and promises to you but also unveils your personal journey with Him. As you leaf through the pages of your journal over time, you'll uncover a personal testament to who He is in your life. It's easy to forget our worth or God's promises when the going gets tough, but your own handwriting will stand as a powerful reminder of your identity and His presence in your life. Then, with confidence, you can proclaim to the world, "I am cherished by the multifaceted God." In Jesus Name, Amen.

Week 19 - Journaling Activity:
Discovering the Many Facets of God

This journaling activity, inspired by the devotion "Exploring the Many Facets of God," invites you to delve into the diverse characteristics of God's nature and how they manifest in your life. Through daily reflection and writing, you'll create a personal record of your experiences with God, celebrating His constancy and the myriad ways He meets you in every season.

Day 1: Jehovah-Shalom, My Peace

- Reflect on a moment when God brought peace into a turbulent situation in your life. How did you experience His peace, and what impact did it have on your circumstances?

Day 2: Jehovah-Jireh, My Provider

- Write about a time when God provided for you in an unexpected way. How did this provision deepen your trust in Him as Jehovah-Jireh?

Day 3: Jehovah-Rophe, My Healer

- Journal about a physical, emotional, or spiritual healing you've experienced. Describe the journey and how you saw God's healing hand at work.

Day 4: Absolute, Unparalleled One

- Meditate on God's uniqueness and supremacy. What does it mean to you that there is none like Him? Reflect on a scripture that highlights this aspect of God's nature.

Day 5: Deliverer, My Rescuer

- Recall a situation where God delivered you from trouble or a difficult circumstance. How did His intervention reveal His character as your Deliverer?

Day 6: Dependable, The Promise-Keeper

- Think about a promise God has fulfilled in your life. Journal about the promise, the waiting period, and the fulfillment, reflecting on God's dependability.

Day 7: Unchanging, My Eternal Foundation

- Consider the significance of God's unchanging nature in a world that is constantly shifting. How does His constancy provide comfort and assurance in your life?

Weekly Reflection:

At the end of the week, review your journal entries. Reflect on the richness of God's multifaceted character and how each aspect has played a role in your personal journey. Identify one characteristic of God that you want to explore or experience more deeply in the coming weeks.

Continuous Engagement:

Keep this journal as an ongoing testimony of your encounters with the many facets of God. Return to it in times of need, adding new reflections, prayers, and insights as you continue to discover more about God's character and His active presence in your life. This personal anthology will serve as a beacon of God's faithfulness, reminding you of the diverse ways He moves and works on your behalf.

WEEK 20 - WEEKLY DEVOTION
UNLEASHING THE INFINITE
IN THE EVERYDAY

Have you ever caught yourself wondering, "Is this too big for God?" If you have, you're not alone. But let's dive into the words of Jeremiah 32:27, where God essentially says, "Challenge accepted!" Imagine God, with a twinkle in His eye, asking, "Is there anything too difficult for Me?" Spoiler alert: The answer is a resounding "Nope!"

Genesis 18:14 gives us a front-row seat to God's promise-delivery service, showcasing that not even the laws of nature can curb His plans. When He told Abraham and Sarah about their next-of-kin arriving in their golden years, it wasn't just a promise; it was God dropping the mic on human impossibilities.

Jeremiah 32:17 and Luke 18:27 serve as divine echoes, reinforcing that the architect of the universe isn't about to be stumped by our earthly dilemmas. It's like God's running a universal "Yes, I can" campaign, and we're all invited to join in.

So, why do we sometimes find ourselves acting like God's capabilities are confined to a box, especially when faced with life's hurdles? It's time to shift our perspective from dwelling on setbacks to scouting for the wonder in our everyday lives. Let's not pigeonhole the Almighty into a "problem solver" role; He's the maestro of miracles, ready to orchestrate the spectacular in our lives.

Feeling swamped by life's challenges? Let's hit the praise button instead of the panic one. Imagine transforming complaints into compliments to God, thanking Him in advance for the victories and breakthroughs. Here's a little prayer to kickstart that gratitude engine: "Lord, You spun the cosmos into existence, so I'm pretty sure you've got my back in this. I'm amped up to see the awesome unfold as you turn my trials into triumphs. You're the undefeated champ, and I'm here for it. Thanks for being the ultimate promise keeper. Amen."

Remember, our God isn't limited by the tick-tock of time, GPS coordinates, or the size of the challenge. His sovereignty stretches beyond the farthest galaxies and right into the nitty-gritty of our lives. So, whenever those nagging thoughts whisper, "That's impossible," let's crank up our faith volume and declare, "For my God, nothing is too wild or wonderful!"

And for those days when the giants seem to loom a little larger, let's remind ourselves that they're on the brink of becoming wonders. Yes, those very obstacles that seem insurmountable today are tomorrow's testimonies. So, with hearts full of hope and voices ready to praise, let's confidently proclaim, "Bring on the hard stuff; my God specializes in turning the tough into terrific." Cheers to embracing the boundless, the beautiful, and the downright miraculous. In Jesus' name, Amen.

Week 20 - Journaling Activity:
Embracing the Infinite with God

This journaling activity, inspired by "Unleashing the Infinite in the Everyday," encourages you to reflect on the limitless power of God in your life and to shift your perspective from seeing challenges as obstacles to viewing them as opportunities for God to showcase His might and mercy.

Day 1: Recognizing God's Infinite Power

- Reflect on a situation in your life that seems impossible to overcome. Write about how this situation makes you feel and how acknowledging God's question, "Is there anything too difficult for Me?" can change your outlook.

Day 2: Witnessing God's Promises

- Think about a time when you witnessed God fulfilling a promise in your life or the life of someone you know, similar to the promise made to Abraham and Sarah. Journal about this experience and the impact it had on your faith.

Day 3: Marveling at God's Creation

- Spend some time outdoors or by a window where you can observe nature. Reflect on the vastness of God's creation and write about how this visual reminder reinforces the belief that nothing is too difficult for God.

Day 4: Transforming Complaints into Praise

- Identify a current complaint or frustration in your life. Write a prayer of praise, thanking God for His presence in this situation and for the victory and breakthroughs that are coming.

Day 5: Envisioning Victory

- Imagine God turning your current challenge into a triumphant victory. Write about what that victory looks like and how it feels to witness God's power transforming your situation.

Day 6: Declaring God's Sovereignty

- Write a declaration of faith, acknowledging God's unlimited power and sovereignty over every aspect of your life. Include specific areas where you need His intervention and express trust in His ability to work wonders.

Day 7: Celebrating God's Faithfulness

- Reflect on the ways God has been faithful to you throughout your life. Create a list of specific instances where God has delivered, provided for, or healed you, and express gratitude for His unwavering presence.

Weekly Reflection:

At the end of the week, review your journal entries and contemplate the growth in your understanding of God's infinite power and love. How has focusing on God's ability to turn challenges into victories shifted your perspective on current difficulties? Identify one tangible step you can take to continue trusting in God's boundless capabilities and to live in a mindset of victory.

Continuous Engagement:

Keep this journal as an ongoing record of your journey with God, adding entries as you encounter new challenges and witness God's power at work in your life. Use it as a source of encouragement and a reminder of God's infinite possibilities, especially in moments of doubt or difficulty.

WEEK 21 - WEEKLY DEVOTION
FINDING CLARITY AND COMFORT
IN THE TWO-CHAIR METHOD

This week, I stumbled upon a gem that's turned my morning routine on its head: *2 Chairs – The Secret That Changes Everything by Bob Beaudine*[1]. Honestly, if there was a way to high-five a book for its impact, this book would be nursing a sore hand. Let me give you a little taste of this life-altering read and nudge you (gently, of course) toward grabbing your own copy.

Bob spins a tale that begins with his mom unveiling the mystery of the two chairs to him. Initially, Bob's head was buzzing with questions: Why two? Who's my plus-one? What on earth are we going to chat about?

He lays out Three Simple yet Earth-Shaking Questions:

Does God get the memo on my life's chaos? - Absolutely.

Is my hot mess too hot for Him to handle? - Please, nothing's too spicy for Him.

Does He have a blueprint for my happiness? - You bet.

Bob suggests a revolutionary meeting strategy: grab two chairs and start your day with a divine appointment. "Once you're in that meeting," Bob reveals, "you'll see God isn't just there to nod and smile. He's got plans—big ones—all designed to give you a future filled with hope and brightness."

Let me tell you, in my 33 years of diving into devotions, *2 Chairs* hit me like a spiritual tsunami. Sitting in that chair, I felt the Holy Spirit's presence so tangibly that my only response was to let the tears flow. It's breathtaking to realize that the Architect of the Universe has the kettle on, waiting to sit down and dive deep into conversation with you.

I'd love to spill more beans about the book, but what I really wish is for you to experience this profound connection firsthand. If there's one read (aside from the Good Book) that I'm sending up smoke signals for you to check out, it's *2 Chairs: The Secret That Changes Everything by Bob Beaudine.*

So, why not set up your own two-chair conference with the Almighty? It's a meeting that could change everything.

Week 21 - Journaling Activity:
Embracing the Two-Chair Meeting

Inspired by the devotion "Finding Clarity and Comfort in the Two-Chair Method," this journaling activity is designed to enrich your daily routine with moments of profound connection and conversation with God. Each prompt encourages you to explore the depth of your relationship with the Divine, using the two-chair method as a springboard for reflection and growth.

Day 1: Setting Up Your Meeting

- Describe your two-chair setup. Where did you choose to place it, and why? Reflect on your expectations for your first meeting with God in this sacred space.

Day 2: The First Question - Awareness

- After asking, "Does God know my situation?" journal about the comfort or revelations this acknowledgment brings. How does recognizing God's awareness of your life change your perspective on current challenges?

Day 3: The Second Question - Trust

- Reflect on the question, "Is it too hard for Him to handle?" Write about a situation you're currently facing that seems overwhelming and how trusting in God's omnipotence gives you peace or hope.

Day 4: The Third Question - Future

- Contemplate, "Does He have a good plan for me?" Journal about your dreams and fears for the future and how believing in God's plan for your life affects your feelings towards those dreams and fears.

Day 5: Listening for God's Plans

- Spend your two-chair meeting listening for God's voice.

Afterwards, write about any impressions, thoughts, or feelings you experienced. How do you perceive God's plans for you might differ from your own?

Day 6: Emotional Responses

- Reflect on any emotional responses you've had during your two-chair meetings. Have you felt peace, joy, conviction, or perhaps a call to action? Journal about these emotions and what they reveal about your spiritual journey.

Day 7: Inviting God into Your Day

- Write a prayer or intention inviting God to be an active part of your day, inspired by your two-chair meetings. How do you plan to carry the insights and peace from these meetings into your daily life?

Weekly Reflection:

At the end of the week, review your journal entries. Reflect on how the two-chair method has influenced your relationship with God and your approach to daily challenges and opportunities. Identify one insight or practice you want to continue incorporating into your routine.

Continuous Engagement:

Keep this journal as a companion to your ongoing two-chair meetings with God. Use it to document questions, revelations, and the evolution of your conversations with the Divine. Return to it whenever you need a reminder of God's presence, guidance, and the transformative power of sitting in His presence.

WEEK 22 - WEEKLY DEVOTION
THE LIFE-CHANGING POWER OF JESUS' BLOOD

Leviticus 17:11 introduces us to a divine principle that feels more like a spiritual law of physics: life is in the blood, and this life brings atonement. Fast forward to the night of the Exodus, and we see God instituting a divine safety protocol: the blood on the doorposts acting as a divine "Do Not Disturb" sign against destruction. This was a shadow of the ultimate subscription to divine protection: the blood of Jesus. Unlike the temporary fixes of animal sacrifices, Jesus' blood came with a lifetime warranty for cleansing, protection, and direct access to God.

Back in the day, invoking the blood of Jesus was as common as asking for salt at the dinner table. Church elders would plead it over everything from personal endeavors to national leadership, knowing its unmatched power to safeguard and bless. Revelation 12:11 wasn't just a verse; it was a lived experience, a testament to overcoming through this sacred defense mechanism.

So, as you step into your prayer closet, remember you're walking in with a spiritual Swiss Army knife: the blood of Jesus. It's not just for emergencies but a daily affirmation of victory over sin, sickness, and fear. It's time to generously apply this heavenly solution over our lives, our loved ones, and our endeavors. Watch as it transforms situations, bringing them from shadow to light, as 1 John 1:7 promises.

And if you're ever in need of a reminder of this power, cue up some classic hymns about the blood of Jesus. Let their melodies carry you to a place of strength and assurance, a reminder of the enduring power of His sacrifice.

Jude 1:24-25 wraps it up beautifully, reminding us of God's ability to keep us and present us faultless. Through the blood of Jesus, we're granted a spotless standing before God—not just in the hereafter but here and now.

Week 22 - Journaling Activity: Encountering the Power of the Blood

Day 1: Personal Reflection on the Blood of Jesus

- Reflect on what the blood of Jesus means to you personally. How does understanding its power change how you approach prayer and your spiritual life?

Day 2: The Exodus and Protection

- Meditate on Exodus 12:13 and its significance. Write about a time when you felt God's protection in your life. How can you relate this to the protective power of Jesus' blood?

Day 3: The Blood as Our Victory

- Revelation 12:11 highlights victory through the blood of the Lamb. Journal about a battle you're facing or have faced and how the blood of Jesus can be your claim to victory.

Day 4: Cleansing and Healing

- Reflect on the cleansing and healing power of Jesus' blood. Is there an area in your life in need of this divine touch? Write a prayer inviting Jesus to cleanse and heal with His blood.

Day 5: Covering in Prayer

- Think about the people and areas of your life you want to cover with the blood of Jesus. List them and write specific prayers of covering and protection.

Day 6: The Hymns of the Blood

- Listen to or read the lyrics of a hymn about the blood of Jesus. Reflect on its message and write about how it inspires you or speaks to your current situation.

Day 7: Living in the Light

- John 1:7 talks about fellowship and cleansing from sin.
  Journal about what living in the light means to you and
  how the blood of Jesus enables this walk.

Reflection And Application

At the end of the week, review your journal entries and reflect on how the awareness of Jesus' blood impacts your faith journey. Identify one insight or practice you want to carry forward and integrate more deeply into your daily spiritual life.

Keep this journal as a living document of your reflections on the power of Jesus' blood in your life. Add to it as you continue to explore and experience its transformative power, ensuring that the life-changing impact of His sacrifice remains a central pillar of your faith.

WEEK 23 - WEEKLY DEVOTION
THE KING'S FANFARE
ECHOES WITHIN US

"Arise, shine; for your light has come, and the glory of the LORD has risen upon you." - Isaiah 60:1

How splendidly favored we are, the champions of faith! Imagine this: not only do we bask in the presence of a King, but He's also gone ahead and sprinkled a bit of His stardust on us. As we roll out of bed and step into the hustle and bustle of our daily grind, let's take a moment to truly absorb the magnificence of this new day He's painted just for us. Today, His mercies are as fresh as morning dew, our past blunders have been tossed into the ocean of oblivion, and behold, we stand renewed in His grace. Ephesians 2:10 sings praises of our divine craftsmanship, "For we are God's masterpiece. He has created us anew in Christ Jesus, so we can do the good things he planned for us long ago." How's that for a self-esteem booster?

Our God, in His infinite wisdom and grace, sees beyond our slip-ups. His love isn't a trophy we earn but a gift, freely given, longing only for us to lift our gazes heavenward. Micah 7:18 captures this divine affection beautifully, celebrating God's unparalleled mercy and delight in lavishing us with love that never fades.

Today, let's tune into the jubilant roar of the King that resonates within us. Yes, that royal procession isn't just around us; it's within us, thanks to the Holy Spirit setting up camp in our hearts. So, let's step out with a spring in our step and a hallelujah on our lips, ready to undertake incredible feats in His name. It's time to embody the essence of His kingdom—not in the food we eat or the beverages we sip, but in living out righteousness, peace, and joy in the Holy Ghost.

Rise and shine, folks! Let the inner trumpets blare and the flags wave. It's time to do Kingdom work, armed with the joy and assurance that comes from the King who calls us His own.

Week 23 - Journaling Activity:
Echoes of the King Within Us

This journaling activity, inspired by the devotion "The King's Fanfare Echoes Within Us," invites you to explore the radiance of God's glory in your life, the renewal of His mercies, and the joy of carrying the King's presence within you. Each day, focus on a different aspect of God's light and how it empowers you to live out His kingdom here on Earth.

Day 1: Recognizing God's Glory

- Reflect on Isaiah 60:1 and what it means to "arise and shine" with God's glory in your life. Write about a moment when you felt God's glory was particularly evident in your actions or surroundings.

Day 2: Renewed Mercies

- Consider the fresh mercies God has given you today. Journal about how this renewal impacts your outlook and approach to the day's challenges and opportunities.

Day 3: Embracing Your Identity

- Meditate on being God's masterpiece (Ephesians 2:10). Write about how understanding this identity shapes your purpose and the "good things" you feel called to do.

Day 4: Love Beyond Faults

- Reflect on God's ability to see beyond our faults to our potential. How does knowing God loves you unconditionally change how you view yourself and your mistakes?

Day 5: The Joy of Unfailing Love

- Inspired by Micah 7:18, contemplate God's unfailing love for you. Journal about how this assurance of love influences your relationship with God and with others.

Day 6: The Inner King's Roar

- Think about the Holy Spirit dwelling within you. How does acknowledging this inner presence inspire you to arise, shine, and live out the kingdom of God daily?

Day 7: Kingdom Living

- Reflect on what it means to live in righteousness, peace, and joy in the Holy Ghost (Romans 14:17). How can you embody these kingdom qualities in your interactions and decisions today?

Weekly Reflection:

At the end of the week, review your journal entries. Reflect on how each aspect of God's character and kingdom has manifested in your life over the past week. Identify one insight or revelation that stood out to you and one action step you can take to more fully embrace the King's fanfare within you.

Continuous Engagement:

Keep this journal as a living record of your spiritual journey, revisiting and adding to it as you continue to explore and experience the presence of the King within. Use it as a tool to remind yourself of God's glory, mercy, and love, and how these divine attributes empower you to live out His kingdom on Earth.

WEEK 24 - WEEKLY DEVOTION
THE ADVENTURE BENEATH OUR FEET

"Every place that the sole of your foot will tread upon I have given to you..." - Deuteronomy 11:24

Who knew a trip to the reflexologist could turn into a divine appointment with footnotes? For years, I've been visiting this foot guru, learning how my footsies can spill the beans about my overall health. Initially, the idea that my feet were more than just transportation seemed wild—like discovering your old car could time travel.

During one particularly eye-watering session (where my reflexologist seemed to press a button that launched me to the ceiling), I had a moment of clarity. The Holy Spirit chimed in, "Everywhere your foot lands, there you are, in full. Your steps carry power, leading you to both divinely appointed and personally chosen destinations." Talk about walking with purpose!

God's message was clear: To truly possess something, we've got to embrace it fully—not just with our arms, but with our thoughts, hearts, and yes, even our feet. Our steps carry our dreams, our fears, and our prayers. It dawned on me that I'd been tiptoeing around God's promise in Deuteronomy, not realizing the spiritual journey I embark on with every step.

Psalm 119:133 became my new morning anthem: "Order my steps in Your word..." It's a reminder to walk in sync with God's beat, exploring paths He's illuminated for us.

So, as we sketch out our plans, let's first check in with the Ultimate Navigator. Where does He envision our feet taking us today? It's about trading our itineraries for His divine GPS settings. By aligning our wanderings with His will, we become conduits of His love and agents of encouragement. It's in the journey on His pathways that we encounter the ordained adventures designed just for us.

To all fellow travelers reading this, let's lace up for a mission beyond mere movement. Our steps, ordered by His Word, have the potential to weave His presence into the tapestry of the everyday. We're called not just to walk but to tread upon promises, leaving footprints of faith that mark the way for others to follow.

As I wrapped up this reflection (and went off to battle the plaque with floss and brush), a final whisper from the Holy Spirit underscored the mission: "I wish to employ not only the soles of your feet but also your voice in the grand endeavor of expanding My kingdom on Earth."

In a world eager for direction, let's be the ones who walk confidently in His promises, guiding others to the light with every step we take. Here's to the journey ahead, paved with purpose, promise, and perhaps a bit of divine reflexology.

Week 24 - Journaling Activity:
Walking in Divine Purpose

Inspired by "The Adventure Beneath Our Feet," this journaling activity invites you to explore the spiritual significance of your daily steps and the paths God has ordained for you. Reflect on the power of walking in alignment with God's will and how each step can be a testament to His promises and plans for your life.

Day 1: The Significance of Steps

- Reflect on the concept that "every place the sole of your foot treads will be yours." What does this promise from Deuteronomy 11:24 mean to you personally? Write about a time you felt God leading you to step into a new area, physically or spiritually.

Day 2: Embracing with Your Heart

- Consider the idea of embracing God's plans with your thoughts and heart. Journal about a dream or goal you're holding in your heart. How can you align this dream more closely with God's word and promises?

Day 3: Steps Ordered by the Word

- Meditate on Psalm 119:133, "Order my steps in Your word..." Write a prayer asking God to guide your steps according to His will and to show you the path He desires for you to walk today.

Day 4: Reflections on Reflexology

- Think about the connection between your physical steps and spiritual journey. How can caring for your physical self help you be more prepared and open to where God wants to lead you?

Day 5: Walking in Divine GPS Settings

- Reflect on the idea of swapping your personal itinerary

for God's divine GPS. What personal plans do you need to surrender to God? Write about the freedom and fear that comes with surrendering your path to Him.

Day 6: Your Role in Expanding His Kingdom

- How can the steps you take today extend God's kingdom on Earth? Journal about specific ways you can use your actions, words, and influence to spread God's love and truth in your immediate surroundings.

Day 7: Leaving Footprints of Faith

- Reflect on the legacy of faith you want to leave through your steps. How can you make your daily walk a testament to God's faithfulness and promises? Write about practical steps you can take this week to leave footprints of faith for others to follow.

Reflection And Application:

At the end of the week, review your journal entries. Reflect on how recognizing the spiritual journey beneath your feet changes your perspective on daily life and decision-making. Identify one insight from this week that you want to carry forward and one action step you can take to walk more intentionally in the path God has for you.

Keep this journal as a guide and reminder of your journey with God. Return to it whenever you need encouragement to walk in His ways and remember that each step you take is part of a greater adventure He has planned for you.

WEEK 25 - WEEKLY DEVOTION
EMBRACING THE DYNAMIC DUO:
COUNSEL AND MIGHT

Rise and shine! As we rub the sleep from our eyes and step into the day, let's invite the Holy Spirit for a refreshing morning breeze that doesn't just tousle our hair but fills us to the brim, empowering us to sprinkle a little bit of heaven wherever we tread. Today, we're diving into Isaiah 11:2, where we're introduced to a celestial team-up that would put any superhero duo to shame: the spirit of counsel and might.

Imagine having a hotline to the divine, offering stellar advice on tap. That's the Holy Spirit for you, ready to guide us towards decisions that sparkle with wisdom. Let's cozy up with Proverbs 15, where we find that "Plans fail for lack of counsel, but with many advisers they succeed" (Proverbs 15:22, NIV). It's like saying, "Hey, two (or more) heads are better than one," especially when one of those heads has access to celestial insights.

Now, let's talk about "might" – it's not just about flexing spiritual muscles. It's tapping into a heavenly power source that could light up the cosmos. Ephesians 6:10 doesn't mince words: "Finally, be strong in the Lord and in his mighty power." It's a call to suit up in divine armor, ready to tackle life's battles with supernatural strength and a strategy straight out of heaven's playbook.

Pairing counsel with might is like having the ultimate life hack. It transforms us from being hesitant to share our wild ideas and dreams into seeking godly wisdom without reservation. Remember those times you kept your visions to yourself, fearing they'd be too out there? With the spirit of counsel and might cheering us on, we find the courage to open up, discovering that sharing could unfold new perspectives we hadn't even dreamt of.

When we align our plans with God's Word and invite His counsel into our decision-making, victories aren't just possible – they're promised. Our supernatural supporter is always in our corner, ready to save, deliver, rescue, and restore.

And as we journey, embracing the spirit of counsel and might, we'll find our paths lined with divine advice and unstoppable energy. It's about living with the confidence that God's goodness and mercy aren't just following us – they're leading the parade. And the best part? This is only the beginning. With God as our host, we're guaranteed a lifetime ticket to His everlasting home.

So here's to stepping out with the dynamic duo of counsel and might by our side. Let's make today a testament to heavenly wisdom and power, walking in assurance that with God, every step is a step towards victory. Amen and amen!

Week 25 - Journaling Activity: Walking with the Spirit of Counsel and Might

This journaling activity, inspired by "Embracing the Dynamic Duo: Counsel and Might," invites you to explore the impact of heavenly guidance and strength in your daily life. Through introspection and reflection, discover how the Holy Spirit's counsel and might can transform your decisions, actions, and outlook.

Day 1: Recognizing the Holy Spirit's Presence

- Reflect on a recent situation where you felt the Holy Spirit guiding you. What was the circumstance, and how did you discern His presence? Write about the outcome of following this divine counsel.

Day 2: The Power of Godly Advice

- Consider Proverbs 15:22's insight on the value of many advisers. Journal about a time when seeking advice from godly friends or mentors provided clarity or a new perspective. How did their counsel align with the Holy Spirit's guidance?

Day 3: Tapping into Divine Might

- Ephesians 6:10 encourages us to be strong in the Lord's mighty power. Write about an instance where you experienced God's strength in a challenging situation. How did relying on His might change the outcome?

Day 4: Sharing Your Vision

- Reflect on a dream or vision you've hesitated to share with others. What holds you back? Journal about how the spirit of counsel and might could empower you to open up and seek godly feedback.

Day 5: The Intersection of Counsel and Might

- Think about how the spirit of counsel and might work together in your life. Write about a decision or action step you need to take, and how you can use both divine guidance and strength to move forward.

Day 6: Witnessing God's Goodness and Mercy

- Meditate on Psalm 23:5-6 and its promise of God's enduring kindness and presence. Journal about how you've seen God's goodness and mercy in your life, especially in times of decision-making and challenges.

Day 7: Your Commitment to God's Path

- Reflect on your desire to walk in the path God has ordered for you. Write a prayer or commitment to seeking the Holy Spirit's counsel and relying on His might daily, asking for the courage to follow where He leads.

Reflection And Application:

At the end of the week, review your journal entries and consider how the themes of counsel and might have resonated with your experiences. Identify one insight you've gained about the importance of divine guidance and strength in your life. Determine one practical step you can take to more actively seek the Holy Spirit's counsel and rely on His might in the week ahead.

Keep this journal as a spiritual roadmap, returning to it whenever you need reminders of God's promise to guide and empower you. Let it serve as a testament to the journey you're on with the Dynamic Duo of counsel and might by your side, guiding you to victory.

WEEK 26 - WEEKLY DEVOITION
TUNING IN TO WISDOM'S FREQUENCY

Kicking off the day without the Holy Spirit is like trying to navigate a ship without a compass—possible, but why make life harder? He's basically our spiritual Google Assistant, ever-present and just waiting for us to say, "Hey Holy Spirit, need a bit of guidance here!" When Isaiah 11:2 mentions the "spirit of wisdom," I picture wisdom not just as a gentle whisper but as a roaring call to action in our lives.

Here's a thought: every morning, I petition the heavens for a wisdom download. Proverbs 8 is my go-to, a divine TED Talk on the virtues of wisdom and understanding. Seriously, give it a read—it's like finding the cheat codes for life.

You've probably heard the adage, "Pray or worry, don't do both." It's catchy, right? But embracing that mantra requires a hefty dose of wisdom. Proverbs 4:7 throws down the gauntlet: "The beginning of wisdom is this: Get wisdom. Though it cost all you have, get understanding." (ESV) It's like wisdom is the VIP pass we all need for navigating life's festival.

So, when life throws its curveballs (and oh, will it ever!), the game plan is to hit pause and pray before reacting. It's about giving the Holy Spirit the floor to weigh in on our dilemmas. Find your quiet corner, tune out the noise, and tune in to that still, small voice. It's in these moments that wisdom wraps around us like a cozy blanket, empowering us to make choices not out of panic, but out of peace.

And let's be real: not everyone's going to give your decisions a standing ovation. But when you're synced up with the Holy Spirit's wisdom, you'll stand firm and unshaken, knowing you've got the ultimate backing. Imagine the stories you'll tell —"There I was, at the crossroads, and wisdom stepped in like a celestial traffic cop."

Welcoming the spirit of wisdom into our lives daily sets us up for success in the divine sense, enabling us to navigate our journey with clarity and purpose. So let's make a date with wisdom every morning and watch how our decisions transform from good to God-level great.

Week 26 - Journaling Activity:
Dialing Into Divine Wisdom

This journaling activity, inspired by "Tuning in to Wisdom's Frequency," is designed to help you actively seek and recognize the spirit of wisdom in your daily life. By engaging with these prompts, you'll develop a deeper connection with the Holy Spirit and cultivate a habit of seeking divine guidance for navigating life's decisions.

Day 1: Inviting Wisdom In

- Reflect on how you currently seek wisdom at the start of your day. Write a morning prayer or intention that specifically asks for the spirit of wisdom to guide you throughout the day.

Day 2: Discovering Proverbs 8

- Read Proverbs 8 and highlight verses that stand out to you. Journal about how these verses can apply to your life and decisions you're currently facing.

Day 3: Wisdom vs. Worry

- Think about a recent situation where you found yourself oscillating between praying and worrying. How could seeking wisdom first have changed your approach? Write about steps you can take to rely more on prayer and wisdom in future situations.

Day 4: Seeking Quiet

- Identify a quiet space where you can listen for the Holy Spirit's guidance without distractions. After spending some time in this quiet space, journal about your experience and any insights you received.

Day 5: Wisdom's Impact

- Reflect on a decision where you felt guided by wisdom.

How did this decision differ from others made in haste or pressure? Journal about the peace or confirmation you experienced as a result.

Day 6: Standing Firm in Wisdom

- Write about a time when you made a decision that wasn't popular or well-received, but you knew it was the right choice because of the wisdom you had sought. How did you remain steadfast in your decision, and what was the outcome?

Day 7: Testimony of Wisdom

- Consider how the spirit of wisdom has impacted your life. Write a testimony or story you could share with friends or family about how seeking wisdom has led to positive changes in your decisions and relationships.

Weekly Reflection:

At the end of the week, review your journal entries. Reflect on how actively seeking the spirit of wisdom has influenced your week. What changes have you noticed in your decision-making process? Identify one key insight or lesson learned about the role of divine wisdom in your life.

Continuous Engagement:

Keep this journal as a living document of your journey with wisdom. Continue to add entries as you encounter new decisions, challenges, and opportunities to seek the Holy Spirit's guidance. Use it as a tool to remind yourself of the power of divine wisdom and the importance of inviting it into every aspect of your life.

WEEK 27 - WEEKLY DEVOTION
DIALING INTO DIVINE UNLIMITED WI-FI

I magine this: God's offering us unlimited fellowship—yeah, like the spiritual equivalent of unlimited Wi-Fi. And guess who keeps hitting the 'disconnect' button? That's right, us. He's there, coffee in hand (or whatever celestial beings prefer), waiting for a heart-to-heart, and we're too caught up ticking boxes off our earthly to-do lists to RSVP to His standing invitation.

God's basically asking us to sync our minds with His. Philippians 2:5 nudges us, "Let this mind be in you, which was also in Christ Jesus." He's got these incredible paths for us, scenic routes really, but there we go, insisting on using our outdated maps.

So, here's a thought: why not schedule some 'fellowship breaks' into our day? Just like coffee breaks but infinitely better. Check in with Him, toss your agendas out the window, and tune in to that gentle whisper. He's ready to lead us in a victory march, shower us with love, open doors we didn't even know existed, and basically make our blessings rain dance-style from every direction.

Diving into the scriptures, it's clear God's got a 'no favorites' policy; He's all about spreading the love and blessings evenly. James 1:7 tells us, "Every good thing given and every perfect gift is from above..." and Romans 2:11 echoes, "For God does not show favoritism." How cool is it to know we're all VIPs in His eyes, and all He wants is to hang out with us?

So, let's not miss out on this incredible opportunity for unlimited fellowship with the Father. Imagine going about your day, humming "I am a friend of God," and actually living it out. Because truly, what's better than having the Creator of the Universe as your go-to pal? Here's to upgrading our divine connection and basking in the glow of His perpetual friendship. Amen and pass the celestial coffee!

Week 27 - Journaling
Activity: Connecting with
Divine Unlimited Wi-Fi

Inspired by "Dialing into Divine Unlimited Wi-Fi," this journaling activity invites you to deepen your daily fellowship with God, recognizing His desire for constant communication and the blessings that come with staying connected to the ultimate source.

Day 1: Recognizing Disconnections

- Reflect on what usually distracts or prevents you from spending time in fellowship with God. Write about these 'disconnects' and how you plan to address them.

Day 2: Syncing Minds with God

- Meditate on Philippians 2:5. Journal about what it means to have the mind of Christ and how this perspective can change your daily decisions and interactions.

Day 3: Planning 'Fellowship Breaks'

- Imagine how you can incorporate 'fellowship breaks' into your routine. Sketch out a few practical moments in your day when you can pause, acknowledge God, and listen for His guidance.

Day 4: Listening for the Whisper

- Spend a quiet moment listening for God's still, small voice. Afterwards, journal about the experience. Did anything resonate or come to mind during this time of listening?

Day 5: Embracing the Victory March

- Write about a situation where you need God's victory. How does envisioning God leading you in a victory parade change your perspective on this challenge?

Day 6: Open Doors and Dancing Blessings

- Reflect on the open doors and blessings you've experienced recently. How do you see God's hand in these? Journal your gratitude and any new opportunities you're excited about.

Day 7: Friendship with God

- What does being a friend of God mean to you? How does this relationship influence your daily life? Write a letter to God expressing your desire to deepen this divine friendship.

Weekly Reflection:

At the end of the week, review your journal entries to see how your connection with God has strengthened. Reflect on the changes you've noticed in your attitude, your awareness of His presence, and the quality of your decisions.

Continuous Engagement:

Keep this journal as a living document of your journey to maintain an uninterrupted fellowship with God. Return to it whenever you feel the need to recharge your spiritual batteries, adding new insights, prayers, and revelations. Let it serve as a reminder of the unlimited connection available to you, and the joy and peace that come with dialing into Divine Unlimited Wi-Fi every day.

WEEK 28 - WEEKLY DEVOTION
THE POWER OF SELF-TALK: TUNING INTO GOD'S FREQUENCY

Ever catch your subconscious acting like a rogue DJ, spinning tracks of doubt, fear, and the classic hits of "Woe Is Me"? Or perhaps it's replaying those less-than-flattering reviews from the peanut gallery of your life? If you're nodding along, it's high time for a playlist overhaul.

Here's the deal: it's time to grab those divine promises off the shelf, face yourself in the mirror, and start the pep talk of the century. Yes, I'm talking about the person staring back at you.

God's got this treasure trove of promises just for you. But here's the catch - you've got to truly believe they're yours for the taking, not just decorations on a shelf. Remember the '90s gem, "What is FEAR?" That's right, "False Evidence Appearing Real." And what's the ultimate reality check? The Word of God, alive and kicking when spoken out loud by you, to you.

It's time to remix your self-talk with God's chart-toppers about you: "You are healed," "You're the head, not the tail," "More than a conqueror," that's you. "Blessed in your comings and goings," absolutely. And why? Because you're worth the ultimate price He paid.

So, let's get down to business. Surrender the me-centered agenda, and let's sync up with God's grand design. Encourage yourself in Him. Before you know it, His promises will be your new self-talk soundtrack. Crank up the volume and let your soul hear the truth. Speak life, health, favor, peace, joy, and freedom over every inch of your existence.

Got a challenge? There's a Scripture verse ready to be your comeback. Remember, we're backed by a God with a flawless win record. So SPEAK THE WORD! And while you're at it, let your actions drop the mic too. Because speaking isn't just about words; it's about living out loud in a way that lights up His glory in HD.

So, what are you waiting for? Adjust that mirror, clear your throat, and start declaring God's promises over your life. Because when you tune into His frequency, your life becomes a symphony of victory.

Week 28 - Journaling Activity:
Amplifying God's Promises
Through Self-Talk

This journaling activity, inspired by "The Power of Self-Talk: Tuning Into God's Frequency," encourages you to actively engage with God's promises, transforming your inner dialogue into a powerful affirmation of faith, identity, and victory. By reflecting and writing, you'll discover the transformative power of aligning your thoughts and actions with God's Word.

Day 1: Identifying Negative Playlists

- Reflect on the negative self-talk or beliefs that have been playing on repeat in your mind. Write them down and counter each with a promise from God that speaks truth into that area of doubt or fear.

Day 2: Divine Pep Talk

- Choose a promise from Scripture that resonates deeply with you. Stand in front of a mirror, read the verse aloud, and then write about the experience and any feelings or revelations that emerged.

Day 3: Facing FEAR with Faith

- Consider a current fear or challenge in your life. How does the concept of "False Evidence Appearing Real" apply? Journal about how you can use specific Scriptures to confront and overcome this fear.

Day 4: The Soundtrack of Victory

- Create a playlist of God's promises, writing down verses that affirm who you are in Christ. How do these truths change the way you view yourself and your potential?

Day 5: Surrendering Your Agenda

- Write about an aspect of your life where you need to surrender your plans to God's. How can committing this area to Him and seeking His will first lead to peace and alignment with His promises?

Day 6: Speaking Life

- Choose a situation in your life that needs transformation. Write down specific Scriptures that speak life into this circumstance. Commit to declaring these verses over the situation daily.

Day 7: Actions That Speak

- Reflect on how your actions can reflect God's glory. What practical steps can you take to ensure your life demonstrates the promises of God not just in words but in deeds?

Weekly Reflection:

At the end of the week, review your journal entries. Reflect on how engaging with God's promises and changing your self-talk has shifted your perspective. Identify one key insight or shift in your mindset that occurred this week.

Continuous Engagement:

Keep this journal as an ongoing dialogue with God and yourself. Continue to add new insights, Scriptures, and reflections as you deepen your practice of speaking God's promises over your life. Use it as a tool to remind yourself of your identity in Christ and the power of speaking life into every situation you face.

WEEK 29 - WEEKLY DEVOTION
YOUR INNER VOICE: THE ULTIMATE
PEP TALK PLAYLIST

Ever realized your subconscious is like a radio DJ, sometimes spinning tracks of doubt and "Greatest Woe-Is-Me Hits" on repeat? And let's not even start on the "Critics' Choice" featuring every negative thing ever said about us. If your mental playlist looks anything like this, it's time for a serious tune-up. Grab those divine promises, stand in front of the mirror, and get ready to have a heart-to-heart with your number one fan – you.

God's thrown open the vault of His promises, but it's on us to claim them as our personal anthem. Remember the '90s classic take on FEAR? "False Evidence Appearing Real." That's right, folks, it's time to flip the script with the ultimate truth – the Word of God. Imagine it: God's word, not just thought silently, but declared out loud by you, for you.

He's saying, "You're healed," "You're leading the pack," "You're a world-beater," "Blessings follow you like a shadow," and "You're the righteousness of God." And why? Because He paid the highest price for your VIP pass to freedom. So, let's drop the mic on our own agendas and open our hearts to His master plan. It's about pumping up the volume on God's promises until they drown out the background noise.

Speak it loud enough for your soul to dance to it – health, success, peace, joy, and abundance. Facing a challenge? Pull up

God's promises like your favorite playlist and let them play over the situation. There's a scripture beat for every battle rhythm. Remember, our God's track record is unbeatable; He laid down His life so we could live ours in victory.

So, what's your move? Let's not just speak victory but live it out loud, in high definition, for the world to see. Because when we embody His word, we're not just talking the talk; we're walking the walk, leaving footprints of faith for others to follow. And as you're about to hit 'send' on your day, remember, it's not just about the words you say but the life you live that cranks up His glory to the max. Let's make our lives a hit single of His promises in action.

Week 29 - Journaling Activity:
Crafting Your Victory Playlist

Inspired by "Your Inner Voice: The Ultimate Pep Talk Playlist," this journaling activity is designed to help you tune into God's promises, transforming your inner dialogue from a mix of doubts and fears to a powerful soundtrack of faith and victory. Engage with each prompt to rewrite your mental playlist, ensuring each track resonates with the truth of who you are in Christ.

Day 1: Identifying the Tracks

- Reflect on the current playlist of your inner dialogue. Identify and write down the negative tracks that play on repeat. Next to each, find a Scripture that speaks the opposite truth and write it down.

Day 2: Divine Promises as Your Anthem

- Choose one promise from Scripture that particularly resonates with you. Write about why it stands out and how declaring this promise can change your perspective and actions.

Day 3: Flipping the Script on FEAR

- Think about a fear or challenge you're facing. Write it down and then, inspired by the acronym for FEAR ("False Evidence Appearing Real"), debunk this fear with a Scripture that reveals God's truth about the situation.

Day 4: Your Mirror Pep Talk

- Stand in front of a mirror and speak aloud the promises of God over your life. How does it feel to hear your voice declaring God's truth? Journal about the experience and any emotions or revelations that come up.

Day 5: The Sound of Victory

- Visualize a recent situation where you felt defeated or overwhelmed. Reimagine this scenario with you responding and acting out of the spirit of victory God promises. Write a victory speech or prayer for yourself based on God's Word.

Day 6: Living the Playlist

- Reflect on how you can live out God's promises in your daily life. Choose one area to focus on and write down practical steps you can take to demonstrate your faith in His Word through your actions.

Day 7: Sharing Your Playlist

- Think about someone in your life who could use a pep talk from God's playlist. Write a letter or note to them, sharing a Scripture or divine promise that you believe could encourage them.

Weekly Reflection:

At the end of the week, review your journal entries and reflect on the transformation of your inner dialogue. How has focusing on God's promises changed the way you speak to yourself? Identify one significant insight you gained through this activity and one way you plan to continue incorporating God's truth into your daily self-talk.

Continuous Engagement:

Keep this journal as a living document of your journey towards embracing God's promises fully. Add new insights, Scriptures, and experiences as you continue to discover the power of speaking life over yourself. Use it as a beacon of encouragement, reminding you of your identity in Christ and the victory you have through Him.

WEEK 30 - WEEKLY DEVOTION
FINDING HOPE IN THE HARD PLACES

Ever had a moment that just knocked the wind out of you? Here's mine: Catching a glimpse of my daughter and seeing how addiction had left its cruel mark, turning a once vibrant being into a shadow of her former self. The physical change was jarring, yes, but it was the look in her eyes that truly broke me—the cocktail of hurt, confusion, and, buried deepest, a glimmer of shame. That look sent me plummeting to my knees, not in despair, but to a place where I could hear God's whisper of hope amidst the heartache. He said, "Rise, for there is hope yet."

Standing up, I felt a strength I didn't know was mine. But something had shifted. Suddenly, I saw the world through a new lens—the eyes of those around me. Behind the glamour and the achievements, I found souls aching quietly. So, I took it upon myself to sprinkle a little bit of encouragement their way, armed with nothing but God's promises. And guess what? I began to see sparks of hope ignite where there was once only dimness.

This journey with my daughter, as heart-wrenching as it was, cracked open a door to my calling. I realized God had equipped me to be a beacon for those adrift in the sea of poor choices —be it due to substances, rocky relationships, or the various losses life throws our way. Loss comes in many forms, after all: through breakups, passings, or simply drifting apart. We're masters at masking our pain, but God? He's in the business of setting us free, preparing us for what's next.

My mission became clear: to reach out to those paralyzed by their circumstances, helping them see that this isn't where their story ends. This isn't a period; it's a comma. A pause before something greater. Because no situation is meant to define us— only refine us into the masterpiece God intended. My heart's cry? To guide those stuck in their 'now' towards the amazing future God has in store. After all, every moment of despair can be the first step toward a destiny filled with hope and joy.

Week 30 - Journaling Activity:
Journeying from Heartache to Hope

This journaling activity, inspired by "Finding Hope in the Hard Places," offers a reflective pathway for processing personal pain, discovering hope, and embracing the transformative journey God has for each of us. Through introspection and scripture, find strength in vulnerability and courage in God's promises.

Day 1: Identifying the Hurt

- Reflect on a current or past situation that has caused you significant pain or heartache. Describe the emotions and thoughts associated with this experience. How has this situation impacted your view of yourself and others?

Day 2: The Look of Shame

- Consider moments when you've felt shame or witnessed it in someone else. What does shame communicate to you? Write a letter to yourself or to someone else, offering compassion and understanding in place of judgment.

Day 3: Hearing God in the Pain

- Recall a time when you felt God speaking into your situation of despair or difficulty. What did He say? If you're still waiting to hear, write a prayer asking for His guidance and a word of hope.

Day 4: Strength Found in Kneeling

- Think about the strength that comes from surrendering to God in prayer. How has prayer shifted your perspective or situation? Journal about the power of prayer in transforming hurt into healing.

Day 5: Sparks of Hope

- Reflect on a moment when you noticed a spark of hope in yourself or someone else during a tough time. What caused that hope to ignite? Write about the role of encouragement and God's promises in fanning that spark into a flame.

Day 6: Called to Comfort

- Have you felt called to support others going through their own struggles? Journal about how your experiences have equipped you to offer comfort and hope to others. How can you use your story to help someone today?

Day 7: Redefining Moments

- Consider how your difficult experiences have refined rather than defined you. How has God used these situations to prepare you for what's next? Write about the person God is shaping you to be through your trials.

Weekly Reflection:

At the end of the week, review your journal entries. Reflect on the journey from heartache to hope you've explored through your writing. Identify one actionable step you can take to move closer to the future God has promised you.

Continuous Engagement:

Keep this journal as a testament to your growth and resilience. Continue to add to it as you encounter new challenges, celebrate victories, and witness God's faithfulness in your life. Use it as a reminder that no matter the hardship, hope and healing are always within reach with God by your side.

WEEK 31 - WEEKLY DEVOTION
YOU'RE ON GOD'S PALM PLAYLIST!

Isaiah 49:16 says, "See, I have engraved you on the palms of my hands; your walls are ever before me." Picture this: You're not just a name in God's diary, you're a permanent tattoo on His cosmic palms. He's got us wrapped up, bordered, and snugly fitted right there in His mighty hands. And let's be honest, that's pretty wild to wrap our heads around. But then, we're talking about the God who's the CEO of the universe, armed with unlimited knowledge, power, and an everywhere-at-once presence.

So, how about we give our own hands a look with a fresh perspective? Imagine turning them into a living, breathing Rolodex (for those who remember what that is) of all the people in our lives who need a bit of love and attention. Envision scribbling their names right into your palms and staying tuned to the Holy Spirit's nudges. Maybe it's a call, a quick note, or a surprise coffee run. The key? Tune in and take the leap.

And hey, if they brush you off with a "I'm all good, thanks," no sweat. Patience is a virtue, right? Sooner or later, don't be surprised if they circle back with a story about how your timing was a divine intervention they didn't even know they needed. 2 Corinthians 4:7 puts it beautifully, reminding us that we're just the jars holding the real treasure: the Holy Spirit guiding us from the inside out.

Just one small act of listening and following through can spin the records of lives in directions you never imagined. Yours, theirs, everyone's life gets a remix from that divine DJ booth. So, keep those palms ready and your spiritual ears open. Who knows whose name will pop up on your palm playlist next?

Week 31 - Journaling Activity: Palm Playlist - Tuning Into Divine Nudges

Inspired by "You're on God's Palm Playlist!", this journaling activity invites you to actively engage with the concept of being engraved in God's palms and extending that care to others. Through reflection and action, you'll explore the impact of listening to the Holy Spirit and responding to those divine prompts in your daily life.

Day 1: Engraved by God

- Reflect on the image of being engraved on the palms of God's hands (Isaiah 49:16). Write about what it means to you to be held so closely by God and how this image influences your perception of His care and attention.

Day 2: Creating Your Palm Playlist

- Look at your hands and imagine turning them into a list of names God is placing on your heart—people who might need an encouraging word or deed. Write these names down and briefly note any specific encouragement you feel led to give.

Day 3: Listening for Nudges

- Spend a day in intentional listening mode, seeking the Holy Spirit's guidance on how to reach out to one person on your palm playlist. Journal about your experience, including any hesitations, actions taken, and the outcome.

Day 4: The Treasure Within

- Meditate on 2 Corinthians 4:7, considering the treasure of the Holy Spirit within you. Write about how this treasure empowers and guides you to be a vessel of God's love and power to others.

Day 5: Acts of Obedience

- Reflect on a past instance where you acted on a nudge from the Holy Spirit and saw a positive impact. How did this experience strengthen your faith and willingness to listen and obey?

Day 6: Divine Appointments

- Journal about a time when someone reached out to you in a way that felt divinely timed. How did it affect you? Reflect on how God uses us in each other's lives for comfort and encouragement.

Day 7: Committing to Attentiveness

- Write a commitment to yourself and God about staying attentive to the Holy Spirit's nudges. How will you ensure you remain open and responsive to His guidance in reaching out to others?

Weekly Reflection:

At the end of the week, review your journal entries and reflect on the insights gained through this activity. Identify any themes or lessons learned about the importance of being attuned to God's guidance in serving and encouraging others.

Continuous Engagement:

Keep your journal as a running record of your palm playlist and the stories that unfold from acting on divine nudges. Continue to add names, reflections, and testimonies of God's work through your obedience. Let this journal serve as a reminder of the power of God's love working through you to touch the lives of others.

Closing with Healing Scriptures
Across All Subjects

As we wrap up our reflection on tuning into divine nudges and extending God's care to others, let's arm ourselves with the powerful Word of God. Here is a compilation of healing scriptures across various subjects, serving as a reminder of God's promises of healing, restoration, and peace for every area of our lives:

Physical Healing

- Exodus 15:26
- Exodus 23:25
- Deuteronomy 7:15
- Psalm 103:1-5
- Isaiah 53:5
- Jeremiah 30:17
- Matthew 8:2-3
- 1 Peter 2:24
- James 5:14-15

Emotional And Mental Healing

- Psalm 147:3
- Isaiah 43:25-26
- Philippians 4:6-7
- 2 Timothy 1:7
- 3 John 2

Spiritual Healing

- Psalm 91:16
- Isaiah 43:25-26
- James 5:16
- 1 John 1:9
- Revelation 12:11

Relational Healing

- Ephesians 4:32
- Colossians 3:13

Financial Healing

- Malachi 3:10
- Philippians 4:19
- Deuteronomy 8:18

General Promises Of Healing And Restoration

- Deuteronomy 30:19-20
- Joshua 21:45
- Psalm 107:20
- Psalm 118:17
- Proverbs 4:20-23
- Joel 3:10
- Nahum 1:9
- Matthew 18:18-19
- Mark 11:23-24
- Mark 16:17-18
- John 9:31
- John 10:10

- Romans 8:11
- 2 Corinthians 1:20
- 2 Corinthians 10:4-5
- Galatians 3:13-14
- Ephesians 6:10-17
- Philippians 2:13
- Hebrews 10:23
- Hebrews 10:35
- Hebrews 13:8
- 1 John 3:21-22
- 1 John 5:14-15

May these verses serve as a reminder of God's unwavering presence and healing power in every aspect of your life. Whether you're seeking physical healing, emotional comfort, spiritual restoration, relational reconciliation, or financial breakthrough, God's Word holds the promises you need to stand on.

Dear Reader,

First and foremost, thank you sincerely for embarking on this journey with us through the pages of this devotion. Your decision to invest time and heart into deepening your relationship with God is a beautiful step toward transformation and growth in every facet of your life.

Let us now bow our heads and hearts in prayer:

Heavenly Father,

We come before You with hearts full of gratitude for every reader who has journeyed through this devotion. Thank You for guiding them to this resource and for the seeds of Your Word that have been sown into their lives. Lord, we pray for their health—may Your healing hand rest upon them, restoring and renewing every cell in their body according to Your perfect design.

We pray for their wealth and provision. Father, open the floodgates of heaven and pour out Your blessings in every area of their life. Guide their decisions, and let their hands be diligent and fruitful in all they undertake. Bless their jobs and businesses, Father, making them lighthouses of Your grace and wisdom in the marketplace.

Lord, we lift up their families to You. May Your peace reign in every household, Your love bind them together, and Your protection be upon them at all times. Let their homes be filled with joy, understanding, and support for one another.

We pray for spiritual growth, that they may draw ever closer to You, developing a deeper understanding of Your Word and Your ways. May their faith be unshakeable and their lives a testament to Your goodness and mercy.

Bless them financially, Lord, not just with abundance but with the wisdom to manage, share, and grow what You have entrusted to them. Let them be channels of blessing to others, reflecting Your generosity and care.

In every area of their lives, Lord, we ask for Your guidance, blessings, and growth. May they see Your hand at work in all things, growing in faith, love, and hope.

Thank You, Father, for the honor of walking this journey together with them. May they continue to seek You, find You, and be transformed by You every day of their lives.

In Jesus' name, we pray,

Amen.

Thank you once again for choosing to walk this path of devotion. May you continue to flourish in God's grace, experiencing His profound love and blessings in every step of your journey.

With heartfelt gratitude and blessings,

-    Mama Katie

BIBLIOGRAPHY

Beaudine, B. (2018). *2 Chairs: The Secret That Changes Everything* (pp. 108-109). Worthy.

ABOUT THE AUTHOR

Katie Brown

Known to thousands as Mama Katie Katie and affectionately known to thousands more as Downtown Katie Brown, she has dedicated over four decades to walking faithfully with the Lord and nurturing a profound relationship with God. Born in Mississippi and raised in New Orleans, Katie has carried the rich cultural and spiritual heritage of her upbringing into her extensive ministry. Over the years, she has become a beloved figure, known for her deep commitment to prayer, ability to offer heartfelt encouragement, and skill in sharing messages that resonate deeply with many.

Now residing in Georgia, Mama Katie has significantly impacted her communities nationwide. Beginning in her early adult years, she embraced her calling to serve others through her church and local outreach programs. As her role evolved, she became a spiritual mentor and advisor, often referred to as Mama Katie by those touched by her generosity of spirit.